Praise for *Death Row Chaplain*

"This book shows how one man's life was changed not by iron bars but by a leather book. That book allowed him to open his heart toward the love that God had for him, which changed his life, changed his household, and ultimately changed the trajectory of the future generations of his family."

—Mike Singletary, coach and NFL Hall of Famer

"A riveting, clear-eyed but supremely compassionate journey through one of the darkest corners of the American judicial system. *Death Row Chaplain* compels the reader to a renewed assessment and appreciation of the human potential for constructive, even inspired, change."

—Harry Edwards, PhD, professor emeritus of sociology, UC Berkeley, and consultant for the San Francisco 49ers, the NFL, and the NBA

"Chaplain Earl Smith is a man of real integrity and unusually effective in dealing with inmates in prison. He also has enjoyed great ability in communicating as a chaplain for the San Francisco 49ers and the Golden State Warriors. He is highly socially mobile, being able to deal with the elite athletes in the world and the most notorious criminals. There are very few ministers who have this range of communication abilities, but Earl certainly does."

—Bill Glass, founder of Beyond the Walls, the largest prison ministry in America

"The stories in *Death Row Chaplain* are told not from a political viewpoint but from a pastor's heart. They are real stories about real men who made real mistakes and who need a real God to forgive them. *Death Row Chaplain* will leave you with a refreshing taste of God's grace. A grace that is available not only to those inside a prison with bars, but to those who may sit in the pew next to you, live next door, bag your groceries, or even look back at you in the mirror."

—Dr. Samuel M. Huddleston, assistant district superintendent, Assemblies of God, northern California and Nevada

To: TOM PARKER

DEATH ROW CHAPLAIN

Unbelievable True Stories from
America's Most Notorious Prison

PROV 3:5-6

Rev. Earl Smith
with Mark Schlabach

H

HOWARD BOOKS
An Imprint of Simon & Schuster, Inc.
New York   Nashville   London   Toronto   Sydney   New Delhi

Howard Books
An Imprint of Simon & Schuster, Inc.
1230 Avenue of the Americas
New York, NY 10020

First Howard Books hardcover edition May 2015

HOWARD and colophon are trademarks of Simon & Schuster, Inc.

For information about special discounts for bulk purchases, please contact Simon & Schuster Special Sales at 1-866-506-1949 or business@simonandschuster.com.

The Simon & Schuster Speakers Bureau can bring authors to your live event. For more information or to book an event, contact the Simon & Schuster Speakers Bureau at 1-866-248-3049 or visit our website at www.simonspeakers.com.

Interior design by Davina Mock-Maniscalco

Manufactured in the United States of America

10   9   8   7   6   5   4   3   2   1

Library of Congress Cataloging-in-Publication Data

Smith, Earl A., 1956–
  Death row chaplain : unbelievable true stories from America's most notorious prison / Rev. Earl Smith ; with Mark Schlabach.
     pages cm
  Includes bibliographical references and index.
  1. Smith, Earl A., 1956– 2. California State Prison at San Quentin. 3. Prison chaplains—California—Biography. 4. Church work with prisoners—California. 5. Prisoners—Religious life—California. 6. Criminals—Rehabilitation—California. I. Schlabach, Mark, 1972– II. Title.
  BV4340.S6325 2015
  259'.50979462—dc23

                                                            2015002103

ISBN 978-1-4767-7777-1
ISBN 978-1-4767-7779-5 (ebook)

I dedicate this book to my dad.
He taught me the definition of unconditional love.
My dad was not perfect by the world's standards,
which made him perfect in my eyes.

Also to my wife, Angel:
as I continued to try to figure out what I was supposed to be
as a man, as a husband, and as a father,
you held on and continued to believe in me
and the call God placed on our relationship.

To Ebony, Earl, Tamara, and Franklin: I feel so blessed
that God chose to loan you to your mother and me.
I will always value the lessons I have learned from you.

To my sisters, Betty Jo and Sylvia: you treated
me more like a son than a brother.
Thank you for helping me survive.

To Curtis, little boys have the tendency to want to look up
to their big brothers; I am blessed that in you I
had a big brother worthy to look up to.

To my mother, thank you for the life-lessons you taught me.
As I have gotten older, the more I have come
to value the unique relationship we had.
I now understand that you did your best,
and for that I am thankful.

Contents

Introduction   xi

1. Fighting for Acceptance   1
2. Gang Family   13
3. God's Rebel   27
4. Born Again   39
5. Cell 66   57
6. Geronimo and Huey   69
7. Robert Alton Harris   83
8. Death Row   105
9. The Baseball Experiment   133
10. Chess on Thursdays   147
11. San Quentin Choir   165
12. Forgiveness   177
13. Project IMPACT   195
14. Faith by Numbers   213

Afterword   229
Acknowledgments   237
Notes   239

Introduction

THIS BOOK IS THE NO-HOLDS-BARRED chronicle of my time as chaplain at San Quentin State Prison in California, which many visitors have described as one of the most menacing and frightening places on earth. During my time behind the walls of San Quentin, I counseled murderers, rapists, and thieves. I prayed to God for mercy with twelve men who were executed for their crimes.

In this book, I will take readers behind the scenes of the state execution process and into the death chamber, revealing my dialogues with the execution team members and the secret thoughts of the men who were awaiting their appointment with the gas chamber or the needle. I will share the stories of family members—those of the victims, and those of the inmates about to face the ultimate punishment.

More than anything else, *Death Row Chaplain* is my memoir of a life rescued by God, a complex story of drugs, crime, race, violence, family, faith, heroism, sports, and forgiveness. It is a testimony about the many ways the Lord helped me to fulfill my purpose: help men beyond all other help discover God's plan for their lives.

My personal story—rising from a life of hopelessness, crime, and nihilism to find God and follow His will—speaks to many people who are struggling to keep their faith and find the righteous path in these difficult times. When I chose God, I was rescued from a life of crime, drugs, and gangs. I was called into the ministry and made the decision to become a Christian. I preached my first sermon one year after I was shot six times and left for dead. A few years later, in 1983, at the age of twenty-seven, I walked through the iron gates of San Quentin to begin serving as Protestant chaplain. It was the fulfillment of my promise to God and to my father.

The men of San Quentin and many others struggling with their place in the world face the same dilemma that I did: the choice between the difficult but righteous path and the old, destructive path. Which path we choose when confronted with these moments of decision making will determine the course of our lives—and the two paths are adjacent and unmarked. I'll share the vital lessons that my many years in the prison have taught me about navigating those situations whereby we can go either way. Through the frightening and uplifting stories of condemned men and celebrity athletes, I'll reveal the many ways that biblical principles and God's grace can help anyone recognize when a critical life choice is before him.

I initiated some programs to help inmates with critical choices to make. In 1989, I launched an education program. A number of men wanted to study the Bible and advance in their educational pursuits. Chaplain Harry Howard and I started it in cooperation with Patten University in Oakland, California. The college purchased the books and the professors volunteered to teach the courses. The certificate program has grown into a fully accredited associate of arts degree program, called the Prison University Project. Under direction of the great staff, which is led by Dr. Jody Lewen, the program has far exceeded anything I envisioned when we were trying to give inmates a better understanding of biblical principles. Since the inception of the original course, over four hundred men have received a certificate in religious studies or an associate of arts degree. Education was, and is still, a large part of what I feel the regenerative process must embrace.

I started and managed the prison's baseball team. I founded the prison's choir and helped produce a music CD that brought incarcerated men, correctional officers, and the prison's administrative staff together for the first time. I sat across from Charles Manson, who to many people is the face of pure evil, for a friendly game of chess, and helped negotiate a truce between rival leaders of the Black Panther Party.

In 1995, I helped launch Project IMPACT (Incarcerated Men Putting Away Childish Things). The program began as a response to two destructive ideas: that men in prison cannot be accountable to one another, and that men of different races and religions cannot coexist peacefully behind bars. Today, this project remains one of my deepest passions. We expanded its influence into the community to curb youth violence and recidivism among ex-cons.

I have been blessed. I have a loving wife and four beautiful children. I was named 2000 National Correctional Chaplain of the Year. In addition to my prison work, I have served as team chaplain for the NFL's San Francisco 49ers, NBA's Golden State Warriors, and Major League Baseball's San Francisco Giants, the first two of which I still work for today. In that role, I've helped some of the world's greatest athletes navigate the pressures of fortune and fame.

However, nothing has filled my soul or shaped the person I am today as much as my time at San Quentin, the so-called Bastille by the Bay. In these pages, I will finally share the deepest secrets, most inspiring stories, and most heartbreaking tragedies of those years.

In imparting twenty-three years' worth of incredible tales from one of the most pitiless environments on earth, I will shine a light on the realities of life in a maximum-security penitentiary: brutality, racism, and despair but also humor, friendship, and hope. I will also share the shocking events that occurred only five months into my tenure as chaplain that shook me to the core, and made me question whether I was worthy of the task God had set before me. I'll expose one of the most mysterious, misunderstood environments in human society—the maximum-security prison—and show that even in a place of violence, racism, and despair, God's love and mercy can still win the day.

I hope to debunk some of the misconceptions I suspect many hold about prison life: that it's 24/7 lockdown, that it's a place of un-relenting physical ugliness, that the inmates are all mindless thugs. I hope by writing this book, I will change your beliefs not only about life behind bars, but about what God's love can accomplish.

1

Fighting for Acceptance

Looking back, I realize now that a career in prison ministry probably appealed to me because I wasn't much different from the inmates. In many ways, I was very much like the men and women whom society has cast aside for their crimes and mistakes. When I was younger, I wanted only what many of them are seeking: acceptance, attention, and love.

I came into the world fighting for acceptance, really from the day my parents brought me home from the hospital after my birth on January 29, 1956. I grew up on the east side of Stockton, California. We had a small house on Scotts Street, where I lived with my parents, Addie and Curtis Smith, and my sisters, Betty Jo and Sylvia, and brother, Curtis. My mother was a very peculiar person, and it didn't take long for me to realize that she didn't love me. I figured out that the best thing I could do was stay out of her sight.

When I was four years old, I was sitting in our living room with my mother and some of her friends. A newborn baby was sitting on one of the women's laps. I realized the bottle was empty. "That baby ain't got no milk," I said.

All of a sudden, my mother turned and slapped me across the face. "Shut up, fool!" she shouted.

I was a little kid, so I didn't know that babies sometimes suck on the nipples of empty bottles to pacify them. I was only trying to help, but my mother embarrassed me in front of her friends. Unfortunately, it is one of the most indelible memories of my childhood. It seemed like every time I tried to get close to my mother, something happened to push me away.

A Great Friend: Ossie

I realized when I was very young that my mother was always going to give the love and affection I so desired to someone else. Fortunately, my parents had hired an older woman, Ossie Pittsfield, to care for me when I was a baby. On the day my parents brought me home from the hospital, my mother handed me over to Ossie. She knew that I needed love, and she gave me every ounce of affection she had. She was one of the most influential people in my life, because she taught me how to love others. In many ways, Ossie rescued me from what would have been an otherwise miserable childhood.

Ossie lived in our house. I slept in a bedroom with her, she fed and bathed me, and spent more time with me than my mother ever did. On special occasions, I rode the bus with Ossie to visit her brother Roy, who worked as a porter on a train that came through town a couple of times a year. She packed Roy a big lunch, and we spent a few hours with him at the train station until he left for another adventure.

When I was six or seven years old, I came home from school and Ossie wasn't there. My mother told me she had sent her packing. I was devastated and so angry. I went door to door in our neighborhood, frantically searching for Ossie, even though my mother had warned me not to do so. I found her living at a friend's house a couple of blocks away; she'd rented a room there so she would be close enough to check on me. When my mother found out I'd been looking for Ossie, she spanked me for disobeying her. It didn't stop me from going back to Ossie's house the next day and many days thereafter.

In many ways, it was at this point in my life at which I stopped caring. If my mother was determined to take away the person who mattered most to me, I didn't think there was much in the world worth living for. From that point forward, I took a turn for the worse and rebelled against my parents and any other authority figures.

As I grew older, though, I began to realize that my mother was incapable of loving me. I've learned over the years that, if people know better, they typically do better. I don't think my mother had the capacity to raise me. When I was older, I learned that my mother had been married to another man when she was very young; he had been physically abusive. My mother ran away from him and his family and fled from Texas to California with her mother. My mom wasn't even sixteen years old at the time.

After she married my father, I was the youngest of their four children and, by the time I was born, my mother apparently wasn't interested in raising another child. I hated my mother then for not loving me, but she didn't know any better. She gave whatever love she had to my older brother, which made me resent her even more and made me very envious of Curtis. At the age of fifteen, Curtis fathered a child, and I watched as my mother poured all of her love and affection on my nephew.

A Good Dad

I was much closer to my father, who loved me and was my protector. My father was the man of the house, and when he was home my mother tended to leave me alone. My father was born in Horatio, Arkansas, and served in the U.S. Navy during World War II. After being discharged from the Navy, he worked for twenty-eight years at the Sharpe Army Depot near Lathrop, California, which is a military distribution and storage facility. My father often had three jobs at once to make ends meet, as he also worked as a mechanic and at a local cannery. He was president of the local American Federation of Government Employees union, which gave him a tremendous amount of pride and power. Politicians would come to our house to talk with my father about getting votes. The majority whip in the U.S. Congress, John McFall, was one of his closest associates.

Even though my dad wasn't home much, he still found time to serve as my Scoutmaster in the Boy Scouts and coach my Little League Baseball teams. He taught me how to fish and hunt. My dad was the superintendent of our Sunday school, and a choir director and trustee at our church. He instilled the importance of education in my siblings and me from an early age. My father was a high school graduate, took a lot of courses from the University of California–Berkeley, and even taught courses on labor relations. He made sure every one of his children did well in school and knew what was happening in the world. He made each of us read the newspaper and to have a report ready for him when he got home. Eventually, all of his children earned college degrees.

One of the most frightening episodes of my childhood was when my father was hospitalized for nearly a month. I was around twelve and too young to realize it at the time, but my father was an alcoholic. I had seen him drinking, but it grew progressively worse. My father had ulcers on his liver, and surgeons had to intervene. It seemed that his entire body was poisoned by alcohol. I was devastated that my dad wasn't home. My mother wouldn't take me to the hospital to see him, so I called him every night to make sure he was okay.

One day, I persuaded one of our neighbors, Mr. Holloway, whom the neighborhood kids called "Old Dude," to take me to see my dad at the hospital. I brought along our family dog, Duke, an enormous German shepherd. My dad loved Duke and took him nearly everywhere he went. He often put Duke in the front seat of his car and put a hat on his head, so that all the kids in our neighborhood would see him.

When Mr. Holloway took Duke and me to the hospital to see my dad, I walked up to the window of his first-floor room. I put Duke's paws on the windowsill and knocked on the glass. My dad saw us and started crying. I didn't know it, but the doctors had told my dad he probably wasn't going to live. When I later heard my mother talking to her friends about my dad's condition, I took his gun and hid it under my bed. It was a pearl-handled Smith & Wesson .38 revolver. I figured if my dad died, I was going to kill myself. I knew there wouldn't be anyone left to care for me. I also knew I needed a gun to protect myself if my father wasn't around.

Thankfully, the doctors were able to save my father and he lived to be eighty-two years old.

Over Time, More Understanding

When I was twenty-six, my parents divorced. My parents believed that I would be happy they were splitting up, but I actually wished they'd remained married. I was really sad, because I wanted my children to see them intact. After all I've told you, you may wonder why. There's more to the story.

My mother and I are not as close as I am sure both of us would like, for many reasons, what transpired during my childhood, and how I chose to live my life. But she's my mom. Do I wish I had a better relationship with her? Of course.

My mother celebrated her eightieth birthday at the house in which I grew up. As I walked through the door, the videographer asked me, "Who are you, and what relationship do you have with Addie?" I told him I was her son. He said, "Yeah, a lot of people here are her kids, but I would like your name for the video." I realized at that point how many people my mother had affected in a positive way. The people in our house were homeless mothers, women who had been in prison, and ministers. My mother had helped so many during her life and, as I walked through the house,

I thought about my life up to that point, and wondered what I could have done differently.

My mother's attitude toward me has not changed over the years. She still has few positive things to say about me, and chooses to spend time with nonfamily members rather than with my family or her grandchildren. That said, I still come away with the same conclusion: My mother just did not have the capacity to bond with and love me the way I wanted or needed. Of course, this hurt. I even thought that when I had children, she would somehow change and love them the way she didn't love me. That hasn't happened.

When I think of what things I could have done differently, first, I could have fought to develop a true relationship with her. I knew how to fight for everything else I wanted, but I didn't try to have a permanent place in her life. Second, had my actions, the things she heard about me, the people I harmed, and the way I lived my life as a young man been different, perhaps she would have found it easier to display some level of love toward me.

Shortly after I took a job as the chaplain at San Quentin Prison, my father decided he was finally ready to stop drinking. He said he was going to a Veterans Affairs hospital to seek treatment. When we arrived at a facility in Martinez, California, I admitted my father, and Betty Jo, Sylvia, and I attended family therapy with him for the next several weeks. Eventually, my dad became very involved in my children's lives, taking them to school some days, and attending their sporting events. My children always played their best games when my dad was in attendance. I guess they liked showing off for him.

Each of my parents eventually remarried, and my dad moved back to Arkansas. He became the pastor of Mt. Zion United Methodist Church in his hometown of Horatio. Shortly before my dad died on August 21, 2009, my wife and I took our kids to see him. My children went fishing with him and our family had our last fish fry together. It was a good way for my children to remember him.

Siblings

When my father wasn't around during my childhood, my sister Betty Jo was my protector. She loved me and treated me as if I was her child. Betty Jo looked after me, made me study, and always made me feel special. I protected Betty Jo, too. I can remember standing in the parking lot of our church when I was probably only eight or nine years old. One of our friends—we called him "Rabbit"—was picking on Betty Jo and pulling her hair. I ran up behind him and tackled him in front of everyone. My dad must have been proud of what I'd done, because he actually took me to get ice cream after church, and I'm pretty sure Rabbit never messed with my sister again.

When we were much older, I learned that Betty Jo and her husband had gotten into a physical altercation. I was attending college in Dallas at the time, and I jumped on the first plane to Modesto, California. A friend picked me up at the airport, and I found Betty Jo's husband and beat him up. Then I got back on a plane to Dallas and got the heck out of Modesto. Looking back, it was a foolish thing; I had claimed my life was changed, and was studying for a degree in religion at the time. But I'm always going to protect my sisters. They were there to protect me when I needed them most.

By the time Betty Jo was in high school, she was very good at concealing my delinquent behavior from my mother. She took an unbelievable amount of verbal abuse from my mom. I don't think my mother wanted me to be close to anyone. Betty Jo was student body president of her high school, graduated with a perfect 4.0 grade point average, and received a full scholarship to Stanford University in Palo Alto, California. Betty Jo wasn't far from home, but I was heartbroken when she left. She managed to come home a couple of times a month, bringing me books to read and making sure I was getting by.

In a lot of ways, my sister Sylvia was my soul mate. Whenever I was sick, Sylvia was sick. When I was ten, I had the mumps at the same time that Sylvia did.Even when I was away at college, Sylvia and I always seemed to be ill at the same time.

As I said earlier, my brother, Curtis, was my mother's favorite son. They were always doing things together. I never understood why my mother liked spending so much time with my brother and not me. It was partly my fault, because I wouldn't have wanted to associate with the kind of person I became when I was older. Curtis was a really good athlete, and he probably could have played college baseball, if not in the Major Leagues. He didn't like to do the things I liked to do, which were hunting and fishing with my dad and running the streets.

My First Brush with an Execution

Curtis and I shared the same bedroom until he left for the Air Force after graduating from high school. We spent many nights talking about life, the way kids do. We had a transistor radio that we hid under our bed from our parents. On the morning of January 17, 1962, Curtis and I listened to news reports as the state of California prepared to execute Elbert Carter in the gas chamber at San Quentin Prison. Carter was the son of a Stockton minister and, years later, I would attend college with his brother. I was only five years old at the time, so I didn't have a complete understanding of what was happening. I certainly didn't comprehend the moral and political issues surrounding an execution, but I still have vivid memories of that morning.

Carter was executed for killing a police officer. On the morning of April 22, 1960, a Stockton police officer, George Woehrle, had attempted to arrest Carter at his parents' home. Carter, who was twenty-three at the time, had been searching for work. He was on the eligibility list for employment as a psychiatric technician at the Stockton State Hospital, and had even taken examinations to become a probationary patrolman with the Stockton police department. A good life seemed to be ahead of him. However, Carter had been romantically involved with a younger woman who had given birth to their child, and an arrest warrant was issued for him on charges of statutory rape.

Woehrle picked up Carter at his parents' home and they left in the police officer's unmarked station wagon. At some point, a struggle ensued inside the car and it stopped about three miles from Carter's home. During the criminal trial, witnesses testified they saw Woehrle and Carter fighting, and that Carter shot Woehrle multiple times with a .22 revolver he'd hidden. Carter tried to escape in the station wagon, but three California Highway Patrol officers shot one of the car's tires during a high-speed chase. Carter ran into a nearby home, where he fired at officers before surrendering. A jury convicted him of murder and other crimes, and he was sentenced to death.

A couple of days later, I accompanied my mother to San Joaquin Memorial Mortuary in Stockton to attend Carter's viewing. I cannot say why my mother took me to see the body. My father knew his father, a minister, through the church. It may have just been curiosity; the mortuary was in our neighborhood, and we may have been passing by, and she decided to stop and view the body.

I still remember how dark his skin looked from his dying in the gas chamber. Nobody in my family ever talked about the incident again, and I certainly never brought the subject up with his brother. For whatever reason, it was a huge moment in my life. No one ever talked about it, but I never forgot.

I couldn't have known that it wouldn't be the last time that I would see a condemned man's face.

$\underline{2}$

Gang Family

WHEN I WAS YOUNGER, IT seemed the only way I could grab my mother's attention was to get into trouble. Finding mischief was easy. By the time I was eight years old, Mr. Patterson, the principal at my elementary school, was paddling me on a regular basis for being disobedient. Before too long, our neighbors knew I was a bad kid. I can still remember hearing Popo and Mama Ruby— James and Ruby Henderson, who lived on the corner opposite our house— shouting at me, "Boy, if you don't change your ways, you're going to end up at San Quentin!"

I was a rough and tough boy who really just wanted his mother's love. Since she wholly rejected me, I was determined to find acceptance on the streets. I began stealing when I was about seven years old. It started with small things, such as candy or trading cards, but I eventually made my way to objects that were much bigger and far more valuable.

I can still remember the first time my father caught me stealing. Growing up, I loved baseball, whether it was playing with my friends on a sandlot, or watching the San Francisco Giants and Los Angeles Dodgers on television. Not far from our house was a baseball field at Stribley Park, which hosted games in the California Mexican Baseball League. Baseball was a big part of our neighborhood culture.

A couple of times a week during the summer, I went to the ball field to watch games and try to snag foul balls. Every once in a while, one of the players would give me a broken wooden bat, which I'd take home and repair with nails and black electric tape. One day, when I was eight, I noticed a brand-new bat sitting near a dugout. No one was around, so I grabbed the bat and hid it in the trees. When the games were over and everyone had left the park, I retrieved the bat and hid it near our house.

One of our neighbors, a teenager named Gene, saw me hiding the bat. He told my father I'd stolen it.

"No, I didn't," I told my dad.

"Yes, he did," Gene said. "I can show you."

My dad was so angry he started whipping me in the kitchen. In our environment, getting a whipping was part of how you were reared. If you did something wrong, something that would bring disrespect to your family, you were chastised. Not only that, but if you did something and a neighbor saw it, the neighbor would also whip you and then take you home and tell your parents—which usually meant more discipline. I would get punished for the deed I had done, and then my dad would talk with me about why I got the whipping, and where the choices I was making would lead. In hindsight, now having children of my own, I understand that my father was doing all he could to try to ensure that I survived the neighborhood.

That day, I tried to run away from him, and cut my ankle on a corner of our stove. It was a deep gash, and my dad had to take me to the emergency room to get stitches. I think my father was more upset about my stealing the bat. As I have said, my dad coached most of my Little League teams, and we always had enough baseball equipment around the house to outfit an entire squad.

Years later, we talked about the incident, and my father told me he couldn't believe I had put myself in jeopardy by stealing something as trivial as a bat. My dad was scared that I was stealing from others at such a young age, and was only trying to save me.

A Bad Kid Gets Worse

Unfortunately, my criminal behavior only grew. Again, when I was eight, I was walking home from school with one of my friends. I found a knife on the sidewalk. I picked it up and stuck my friend Alvin Oliver with it. I'm not sure the knife even punctured Alvin's skin, but it scared him to death. I don't think stabbing my friend with a knife affected me; I didn't feel any remorse for what I'd done. Alvin ran home to tell his mother, and I continued walking home.

Before too long, a police cruiser stopped in the road, and the police picked me up. They took me home and told my mother what happened. By that time, I think both of my parents feared that

I was crazy. My father was really worried about me, because he knew I was a very angry kid. I cannot think of anything my mother said or felt about it. She let my father handle me. However, on this occasion, I remember his talking to me with tears in his eyes, asking what was wrong with me. No whipping this time.

My behavior at school wasn't much better, and my father unknowingly enabled me to act out in class. One day, Mr. Patterson called me to his office and told me to bend over. He beat me fiercely with his paddle. When I went home that day, I told my dad what happened. My father went to the school the next morning, grabbed Mr. Patterson, and started throwing him around his office. He told Mr. Patterson never to touch me again. Their exchange became so raucous that school officials called the police.

After my father went to his office and handled him, Mr. Patterson no longer felt he could get away with the treatment he was giving out. I realized then that my father would protect me no matter what, so I felt free to behave badly. Mr. Patterson never paddled me again.

Some may wonder why, if my father wanted to protect me, he didn't stop my mother from being so hard on me. The major issue with her, though, was not the spanking—it was the mental abuse, which he could do nothing about.

I knew my dad loved me, because of what he did. I realized eventually that his entire life was focused on protecting me. My father later told me he was called to the ministry and my mother told him if he started to preach, she would divorce him. He knew that if she divorced him, she would have me, so he decided forego what he knew God had called him to do for the sake of staying with me. He knew that if he were not around on a regular basis, he couldn't walk me through the issues life would bring my way. He was my protector, because he thought more of my future than of his.

Lines Drawn

As a kid, you truly desire one thing: to be accepted by others. Well, my mother rejected me at home, but I was beginning to find my place at school. There were a lot of African-American kids attending Fremont Junior High School. We were bused from neighborhoods on the east side of Stockton to a school in a lily-white part of town. Stockton, which is located about fifty miles south of Sacramento in central California, has long been an eclectic melting pot of whites, blacks, Mexicans, Chinese, Filipinos, and Japanese.

Long before the Civil Rights Era, school districts separated races in Stockton. The Deep Water Channel and Main Street, which run through the center of town, separated white North Stockton from South Stockton, where most of the blacks and other minorities lived. Through unscrupulous zoning policies, the Stockton City Council protected properties on the north side while opening up the south side to unrestricted land use. As a result, only middle-class or affluent white families could afford to live on the north side of town, while everyone else settled for less costly housing on the south side.

Most of the city's low-income housing was built near the World War II naval base on the south side. Unlawful racial covenants were in place to prevent nonwhites from moving into neighborhoods on the north side. Until the 1950s, there was a city ordinance that specified that Chinese residents had to live south of Main Street!

Two school districts on the north side catered largely to white students: the Lodi Unified School District and Lincoln Unified School District, both of which were more than 80 percent white during the 1960s. When James Reusswig was hired as Stockton's new school superintendent in August 1966, he sought to integrate the schools to make them more racially balanced. Reusswig realized the U.S. government was eventually going to force Stockton to desegregate its schools, and he wanted the city and its residents to do it voluntarily.

However, the school board rejected Reusswig's plan to bus minority students into white school districts, and then the school board bitterly fought a lawsuit filed on behalf of a few minority students. Student riots took place at a handful of the junior high and high schools in town. The situation grew much worse after a white student was thrown out a window of the science class of my junior high school. The black and Hispanic students were gathered in an area on the side of the gym and when the police arrived, we started to run. As we started to run, they released their dogs, and some people were bitten.

Boycotts and Buses

After a long, controversial legal battle, Stockton's schools were finally integrated. I had to take a public transit bus to get to Fremont Junior High for the first couple of years; the school board apparently didn't feel comfortable sending a busload of white students into my neighborhood. On the days I missed the bus, I had to walk four miles down railroad tracks to get to school.

On the way, I had to run through an all-white neighborhood. If I didn't run fast enough, I was usually greeted by a group of older white kids who didn't want me there. Sometimes they would fight with me, sometimes they would throw rocks at me, sometimes they would circle me, push me, and call me names. One time, they came by my house and shot our den window. It was at that time that I saw an amazing side to our community. Certain men—Mr. Russell, Mr. Williams, Mr. Saulsberry, and Mr. Stafford—showed up with weapons ready to defend and protect our neighborhood. I was sad about the shooting but, boy, was I proud of those strong black men.

Eventually, we coerced the school district into providing us with school buses: During one trip to school on city transit, we forced the driver off the bus and staged a boycott. After that, the school district was forced to run its bus routes through our neighborhoods.

Shortly after I enrolled in junior high, I was recognized as one of the leaders of the African-American students in my class. My teachers and school administrators obviously weren't aware of what I was doing outside of school: stealing and selling drugs.

However, as a leader in my class, I was placed in counseling with other black students, which was supposed to help us better understand white people, so that we could relate to them. It didn't work. I didn't trust my white teachers because most of them lived in the all-white neighborhood in which our school was located. I didn't understand why they were allowed to discipline us, especially when it was obvious that they didn't care about us. We were being forced to attend their school in their neighborhood, and they made it clear that they weren't very happy about us being there.

By the time I was twelve years old, I was a rage-filled, bitter young man who hid his pain of rejection behind a façade of violence. By the time I entered junior high, I had become intimately acquainted with the police, the feeling of handcuffs, and the smell of the back of a police cruiser. I had graduated to stealing cars, money, and guns. I broke into homes and businesses and robbed innocent people at gunpoint. Before long, I was smoking marijuana, and selling weed and other drugs.

Fortunately, my dad managed to keep me out of Peterson Hall, the city's juvenile detention center, and rarely mentioned my troubles to my mother. I was another young African-American male on a seemingly one-way journey to San Quentin Prison or worse, a premature death. I was on the preordained path of virtually every young thug in America, a path full of drugs, greed, and violence. I was slowly alienating myself from almost everyone who loved me.

My father stuck with me: He continued to encourage me and speak victory into my life, no matter what situation I was in. He seemed always to believe the best for me. Unfortunately, I was too narcissistic and naïve to realize it at the time.

Gang Life

When I was at my worst as a kid, my sister Betty Jo was attending Stanford University. One weekend, she came home with a friend who introduced me to the game of chess. He brought me a chessboard and patiently explained all of the game's pieces to me. "These are your pawns," he told me. "They're your protectors."

Not long thereafter, I formed a gang with a group of boys from my neighborhood. We called ourselves the Scotty Boys, after the street where most of us lived. By being a part of a gang, I felt as though I finally had a family. Because of my violent behavior, I was revered, respected, and feared in our neighborhood. Others accepted me, even if for the wrong reasons, which was the only thing I ever wanted. More important, others surrounded me, protected me from rivals, and insulated me from the crimes they were often committing on my behalf. In many ways, they were my pawns.

I was living a mean, ugly, dangerous life. I was involved in many violent incidents and thought nothing of destroying others' lives in order to preserve mine. One day, when I was about sixteen, I was standing in front of my house with my father when a car coming down the road swerved quickly as if to hit us. I recognized the two teenagers in the car, a pair of twins. They weren't from our neighborhood; they were there to buy drugs. The driver laughed at us from his window as he sped away. My father ran toward the house to get his gun, but I stopped him before he did something that would get him into trouble.

A couple of hours later, I slipped out of our house and went searching for the guy who was driving. I found him down the street at a neighbor's house. I grabbed a two-by-four and beat him senseless. When I was finished, everyone looked at me as if I were crazy. I dragged the guy up to the railroad tracks and left him there. I wanted a train to run him over and kill him. But he survived. Two guys in the neighborhood saw the whole thing and got him off the tracks after I left.

School Interrupted

Near the end of my ninth-grade year at Fremont Junior High School, I finally snapped. One of the vice principals didn't like black students. During one of the last days of the school year, I was involved in an altercation with a white student. The vice principal put his hands on me, and I protected myself from both of them. Because of my fight with the school administrator, I was sure I'd never be allowed to attend another class in the district. I didn't attend my expulsion hearing.

Several days later, Curtis graduated from Franklin High School, which was another predominantly white school in the district. As Curtis walked across the stage, wearing his cap and gown and holding his diploma, he raised his right fist in the air. He mimicked African-American athletes Tommie Smith and John Carlos, who raised their fists during their medal ceremony at the 1968 Summer Olympics in Mexico City. Although Smith later said that his gesture was a human-rights salute,[1] it became a lasting symbol of the Black Power Movement of the 1960s and 1970s. I'm sure nearly everyone at Curtis's graduation ceremony was shocked by his actions, but I was so proud of him. He was about to join the U.S. Air Force to defend his country, but in the United States he was still being denied civil rights like other African-Americans around the country.

A few days after Curtis's graduation, a vice principal at Franklin High School, George Braun, informed my father that the school administrators didn't want me to attend their school. He even told him that, if I tried to go there, I would be hurt. Amazingly, I was able to obtain a partial scholarship to Saint Mary's, a private Catholic high school in Stockton. Although I was selling drugs and committing violent acts on the streets, I was still maintaining my grades and was a capable student. I also was a pretty strong football player on the offensive and defensive lines.

It may seem strange that St. Mary's took me in. I was not thought of as a good church kid; in fact, St. Mary's never considered my church membership or involvement because I was Baptist, not Catholic. The school accepted me because my father worked an extra job to pay the tuition, I passed the academic entrance exam, and I was a decent athlete. At the time, black students made up about twenty in an enrollment of over eight hundred. For the most part, the male students were athletes who could also handle the tough academic requirements associated with a college prep institution.

Drug Runner

The head football coach at Saint Mary's High helped me get a job at his brother's pharmacy. Can you imagine that? I now had access to every kind of prescription medicine—the regulations and records weren't the way they are today—and the pharmacy provided me with a car to deliver prescriptions, customer orders, and, without their knowledge, recreational drugs to my customers and dealers.

Saint Mary's High School also provided me with a much more affluent customer base, as most of my classmates came from the wealthiest families in the city. I started by selling small quantities of weed, like matchboxes for five dollars and sandwich baggies for twenty dollars, I then moved to moving bricks and pounds of marijuana. I knew students who preferred cocaine and heroin, and others who liked prescription pills.

Parents complained that I was selling their kids drugs. Every few months, a couple of police cruisers would pull up in front of the school. A few minutes later, I would be called to Father Thomas O'Neill's office over the loudspeaker. "Hey, we know what you're doing," he told me. "You're embarrassing yourself and us. Stop before you ruin your life." Sadly, Father O'Neill's advice fell on deaf ears. I never brought drugs to the school, so police never found anything when they searched me.

I tried to keep my drug enterprise away from the high school as much as I could, but I continued selling drugs when I wasn't in class or at football practice. Even though I was in a minority at the school, I was popular among my classmates and managed to stay out of trouble. I was elected vice president of the student body before I graduated in the spring of 1974.

Graduation Surprise

I'm certain my parents were afraid I'd never graduate because of my extracurricular activities. But I pulled it off. My dad told me that my graduation day was one of the proudest of his life. When my brother graduated from high school, my mother bought him clothes and a Ford Pinto as graduation gifts. She threw Curtis a big party and invited all of our family and friends. It was a celebration.

When I graduated, I had to borrow my dad's jacket and tie to wear in my graduation pictures. My mother bought me a suitcase, which she promptly put in my bedroom.

I had already decided that I was finally getting away from my mother no matter what, but you always remember what your parents give you for graduation. My mother's message to me on that day couldn't have been clearer. Still, I couldn't wait to get out the door.

I didn't know, though, which direction my life was going to take.

3

God's Rebel

MOST AMERICAN BASEBALL FANS PROBABLY remember October 22, 1975, as the night the Cincinnati Reds defeated the Boston Red Sox 4–3 at Boston's Fenway Park to win one of the most dramatic World Series ever played. Game 7 of the 1975 World Series, which the Reds won on Joe Morgan's run-scoring single with two outs in the top of the ninth inning, seemed anticlimactic compared to the game that was played the night before.

In Game 6, Red Sox catcher Carlton Fisk hit a dramatic twelfth-inning home run in which he famously tried to wave the ball fair as he hopped down the first base line. Not until Fisk's walk-off homer clanged off the left-field foul pole above the Green Monster did the Red Sox know they'd escaped defeat and lived to see another day in a winner-take-all Game 7. Even to this day, it is probably the most famous play in Major League Baseball history.

I was a sophomore at Stanislaus State College in October 1975. President Gerald Ford was in the White House. The Vietnam War had only recently ended, and the Viking 1 spacecraft was well on its way to the first landing on Mars. I remember watching Fisk's dramatic home run on television in my apartment near my parents' home.

I had planned to watch Game 7 of the World Series, but I ended up fighting for much more than the Reds and Red Sox that night. When Morgan slapped his game-winning single into center field to lead the Big Red Machine to victory, I was lying in a hospital bed covered in blood and fighting for my life.

Extracurricular

After graduating from high school, I'd enrolled in classes at Stanislaus State College in Turlock, California, which is located about forty miles south of Stockton. My sister Sylvia was already attending college there, so I figured it would be a great place to start life on my own. Of course, Stanislaus State afforded me a much bigger market in which to sell drugs, and I spent a lot of time driving back and forth between Turlock and Stockton to service my dealers and customers. I had a home in each town.

During my freshman year of college, I shared an apartment with a classmate from Saint Mary's High School, Rupert Cooper, who was a really square dude. He had no idea I was dealing drugs in high school, so he started wondering why I had so many friends coming through our apartment at all hours of the night. Finally, I had to tell him. I even showed him where I was hiding the drugs in our apartment in case the police raided our place.

When I came home from classes one day, Rupert said, "Hey, man, I took care of it for you."

"Took care of what?" I asked him.

"A guy came by to buy some drugs, and I sold him some weed," Rupert said. "I thought you sent him to get it."

I was flabbergasted. I couldn't believe Rupert sold drugs to someone he didn't even know. I was convinced I was under surveillance by the local police, and I was afraid they'd sent an undercover cop to our apartment to make a buy. After that incident, I became super paranoid. I threw away all the drugs in the house in Turlock.

It turns out the police weren't watching me as closely as I had feared, and I continued running my drug operation throughout my freshman year. I breezed through my courses and returned to the school the next fall after spending the summer between Turlock and Stockton.

Before I watched the Red Sox win Game 6 of the World Series, I went to my parents' home to check on my dad. My father was my friend and I tried to check on his drinking and his stability as often as I could. Sometimes, the lifestyle I was leading kept me away from him. When I was in the area and thought he was home, though, I would drop in.

During this particular visit, my mother told me about a dream she'd had the night before and said that if I didn't stop what I was doing, I was going to be killed. It was one of the few times in my life that my mother showed a genuine concern for me. It was the closest that she ever came to worrying about me. My girlfriend at the time was so upset by what my mother said that she cried. I lived across the street from my parents and next to my grandmother, and they were all concerned. But I didn't put much stock in what they were saying. I was nineteen years old and knew how everything worked.

Untouchable

The police in Stockton had been trying for years to find a way to bust me. They knew I was a criminal, but they couldn't prove it. I was living a double life: I was going to college and keeping my nose clean in public, while running a vast network of drug dealers in multiple cities from my apartments. I had become increasingly violent and brazen as my drug network grew larger. I knew I had to protect what I considered my turf and wasn't afraid to hurt others who infringed upon it.

One night, as I was driving through a neighborhood with my girlfriend, I saw a guy who had ripped me off. He had been selling drugs for me and decided not to pay me the money he owed. He thought because he was older than I was, he could just get away with publicly disrespecting me. He tried to steal two things—the drugs and my reputation.

I stopped my Ford Fairlane and walked to the back of the car. I took a shotgun out of the trunk. I drove back by the guy and fired a shot. I knew I was too far away to kill or seriously wound him, but I wanted to make sure he received my message: I knew what he'd done. My girlfriend started screaming and hitting me. Whenever I did something crazy like that, I tried to make sure no one was with me. I didn't want anyone else to get hurt and, just as important, I didn't want anyone to witness it. As far as I was concerned, I was untouchable.

Firecrackers

The night of October 22, 1975, proved me wrong. It started like any other day. I attended classes at Stanislaus State College in the morning. That afternoon, I met a couple of associates at Van Buskirk Golf Course in Stockton. We liked to talk business on the golf course because the police couldn't snoop on us. My friends and I discussed how we were going to make a big drug deal in the coming days.

When I returned to my apartment, I put my golf clubs in a closet and sat on the couch to watch Game 7 of the World Series. There was a knock at the door. I reached for a handgun I had hidden in my couch, but I forgot that I had put it in my golf bag. There was another gun in my bedroom. (Hey, I told you I was paranoid!)

I saw one of my drug dealers, Michael, at the door. He owed me money, and I figured he was finally coming to pay me. He had another person with him whom I didn't recognize. I thought the guy was a drug buyer; I didn't know Steven Moore was a gang member from Los Angeles and was hiding his father's gun under his shirt.

Michael was a good kid. He was a really skilled athlete, and I knew his mother and father. I had no business dragging him into the drug trade. He owed me money and was scared. He was so afraid that he brought someone to my house to kill me.

After the guys sat down on my sofa, I noticed Michael making a gesture with his hand. Before I could react, Moore pulled out his gun and opened fire. I dove under my coffee table. I foolishly believed the wood would protect me from bullets. (Remember what I said about believing I was invincible?) Moore made his way to the side of the table and stood over me with his gun pointed directly at me. He shot me six times. Up until that point, I knew what it felt like to shoot somebody but hadn't felt what it was like to be shot.

For the record, it feels as if hot pokers have struck your body. The pain is more from the burning associated with the bullet than the impact. My body felt as if it were on fire, and I remember I wanted some cold water to ease the feeling of burning. I can still hear the sounds of his gun firing. When Moore fired the last bullet and kept clicking the trigger, Michael said, "Let's go. He's done." They ran out the front door.

Somehow, I made my way out of my apartment to a stairway bannister. One of my neighbors, Mrs. Lorraine, told me she thought she'd heard firecrackers. She saw me bleeding and called police. I'm sure Ms. Lorraine thought calling the police would get an ambulance to me. I'm not sure anybody thought my life was worth saving. I knew that I deserved to be shot.

As I lay bleeding outside my apartment, a couple of Stockton police officers went inside, then quickly left. They didn't even try to help me. I guess I was only another dying street thug to them. After a second set of police officers came to my apartment, Mrs. Lorraine asked them, "Where's the ambulance?"

"Lady, if you want an ambulance, you call it," one of the police officers told her.

Deathbed

An ambulance finally arrived, and I was transported to the trauma ward at St. Joseph Hospital. I had suffered gunshot wounds to my left cheek, below my nose, right bicep, right leg, as well as my upper and lower back.

A doctor and a couple of police officers greeted me at the hospital. "You're going to die," the doctor said. "At least tell the police who shot you."

I laughed at his suggestion. In my culture you didn't snitch, even if you were on your deathbed. I was so entrenched in my lifestyle and what I was doing that even though I was dying, all that mattered to me was my reputation and credibility on the streets. More than anything, I was in disbelief that someone had been fearless enough to shoot me. I remember thinking: *You don't shoot me. I'm Smitty. Nobody does that to me.*

The doctor, James Morissey, shook his head after my response. "I don't understand you people," he said.

My father came to my room a few minutes later. "How bad is it?" he asked the doctor.

"He's not going to make it," the doctor said.

I'll never forget what my father did next. He grabbed the doctor's white lab coat and told him, "Doc, you do what you do best, and I'll do what I do best." Then, my father came to me and said, "Son, you are a rebel, but you are God's rebel. He is going to use you to His glory." Then my dad left my room to be alone with God. He prayed for a miracle.

Voice

I have no idea if what happened next was because my dad was especially persuasive with the Father or because the Lord decided it was time to put His plan for me in motion. What I do know is that as I lay on that bed, with gunshot wounds burning me like red-hot pokers, suddenly my pain stopped. I felt a peace and calmness come over me. Then a voice came to me and said, "You're not going to die. You have things to do. You're going to be the chaplain at San Quentin Prison." The voice was clear and the message was succinct. It was as if I'd come out of the darkness and into the light.

I don't know if I even believed in God at the time. In the church where I grew up, when you reached a certain age, you were expected to accept the Lord and be baptized. When I reached the age of nine, the barber in our neighborhood, whom I called Uncle Nathan, told me I needed to accept Jesus Christ as my Lord and Savior. Uncle Nathan was very concerned about my behavior and the direction of my life. "It's time for you to get saved," he said, "and for you to be baptized."

The following Sunday, I accepted the Lord and was baptized the next week. After church, Uncle Nathan took me to Foster's Freeze on Main Street in Stockton to get ice cream. I was baptized because the adults in my family and in our church expected me to do it—it wasn't because I actually understood what I was doing. I thought it made you a better person, and there's no question I needed to do that. Even at nine years old, I was pretty screwed up. I thought being baptized might help me, but it didn't.

I certainly hadn't paid attention to the Word during my years of robbing, shooting, and drug dealing. My family held tight to a strong Christian faith, and despite my criminal life, I had gone to church regularly since early childhood. So, as I lay on that hospital bed fighting for my life, I understood that it was the Lord speaking to me. What I didn't understand was *why* He was talking to me. Up until that point, I had done nothing in my life to honor my relationship with God; I wasn't worthy of His attention, much less to be His instrument.

Reason to Live

It was my first experience with God's grace. As I now know, grace is God's undeserved favor—the unconditional love He gives to each of us, though we all are sinners. In my youthful arrogance, I didn't understand that it didn't matter if I thought I was worthy of the Lord's attention—He thought I was. The idea humbles me to this day. In an instant, that voice changed everything for me. For the first time in a long time, I had a reason to live—to turn my life around and do something good.

If it was God's way of getting the attention of a cynical, angry young man, it worked. For the first time, I felt God working in my life. At that moment, I knew that He might actually have something in mind for me besides crime and prison—but I had to choose it. In the hospital, I realized there had to be something better than the life I had been leading. I only had to figure out what it was and go after it. As I lay fighting for my life, I stood at the intersection of two paths: one toward God and a life of service and redemption, or back to a life of crime and violence.

After my communion with the Almighty, the doctor came back into my room to check on me. I was laughing because God had told me something that sounded utterly ridiculous. Perhaps it was a combination of shock and amazement that God would speak to me. I think that the doctor thought I was going into shock. He and his team were having a difficult time treating me. I wonder if they were thinking, *what's the point? He's shot up, refuses to talk to the police, doesn't care about his own life, why should we?* My face was swollen and my back and leg had seven visible holes, so they did not even know how many times I was shot or what kind of gun was used. My body was covered in blood.

"Doc, would it help if I told you where the bullets are?" I asked.

The doctor stared while I pointed to the holes in my body. I'm still not sure how I knew where the slugs were located, but I found each of them. As I touched each wound, the bleeding stopped. I needed stiches for only one bullet hole, the one in my face. (The hole in my nose closed up and the bleeding stopped on its own.) Somehow, the remaining wounds closed without sutures. Doctors were able to remove three bullets; two of them are still in me to this day, including one next to my heart.

It's an absolute miracle that I didn't die or wasn't left without the use of my legs. Each of the two bullets fired into my back might have very easily severed my spine, and one of the bullets in my face might have hit my brain. Miraculously, I didn't suffer significant lifelong injuries, only a few scars serving as daily reminders of the night I almost died.

Aftereffects

After being shot six times in an attempted murder, I was sent home after only three days in the hospital. I still faced a long road to recovery, and my father was at my bedside for the duration of my struggle. My mother never came to see me at the hospital. I think she was embarrassed by what happened to me.

I remember waking up in my old bedroom in my parents' home, with my father sitting in a chair holding a gun. He was afraid someone was going to come to our house to finish the job. Once again, my dad was there to protect me. The guys who shot me hadn't been caught, and I still hadn't revealed their identities to the police.

After a couple of weeks of resting at home, I was finally able to get up and move around. One day, there was a knock at the door. It was a couple of my associates from the drug ring. They'd found the guy who shot me and wanted to kill him. One of my friends was the guy's stepbrother, but he was determined to kill him for what he'd done to me.

"No, I have to do it," I told them. At that moment, I did truly intend to kill both of the guys responsible for shooting me. My reputation required that I pay back the guys who had harmed me. For me, payback was simple: death.

But, after my experience with the Lord in the hospital, I knew I couldn't kill him. If the Lord was going to forgive me for my transgressions, I had to learn to forgive those who had harmed me. Besides, I knew I was a very lucky man, not only because I was alive, but also because the police didn't have enough evidence to charge me with a crime. Most of the drugs and money that had been hidden in my Stockton apartment somehow vanished during the frantic moments after I was shot; I'm still not sure who took them.

My sister, Betty Jo, who had by then graduated from law school and would become an outstanding attorney, was able to argue that in this case I was a victim of a crime, which kept me out of jail. My sister knew more about me than anyone other than my father. She knew I was into some very deep stuff, but Betty Jo also believed that I was better than the life I was living.

Moore, the man who shot me, was eventually arrested. He admitted his crime. I went to his trial but didn't testify against him. I watched as a judge sent him away to prison.

As I left the courthouse that day, I thought that it was the last time I would see the man who tried to end my life. I didn't know that God had something else planned for us.

4

Born Again

AFTER I WAS PHYSICALLY STRONG enough to return to my apartment, a good friend came to my front door. His name was Broderick Huggins, and he knew I was going to die if I didn't turn my life around. Even after I'd survived six gunshot wounds, Broderick still wasn't convinced I'd heed a wake-up call to turn away from my life of crime, drugs, and violence.

"Man, I've got to preach tonight, and I want you to go to church with me," he said.

"Okay, I'll be there," I told him, knowing I wasn't about to spend the night sitting in a church pew.

"No, you're going to ride with me," he said. "I'm not leaving unless you come with me."

During Broderick's fiery sermon at the White Rose Church

of God in Christ in Stockton, California, I was reintroduced to Jesus Christ. I listened intently to what Broderick preached and was very moved by his message. That night, I openly and willingly dropped my façade. I acknowledged that I needed help, and that help could only come from Jesus. Unlike the time I was baptized as a boy, I was mature enough to understand what I was doing.

Hearing Broderick's message in the church only bolstered my desire to turn my life around. I wasn't selling drugs anymore—getting shot six times and being left to die had at least scared some sense into me—but I was still heavily involved in the things that came with drugs. The parties, the gambling, the women: the lifestyle was an adrenaline rush, a drug, and I was addicted. Living the street life is like digging a hole. The farther in you go, the more work is necessary to get out. I could not just quit what I was doing. Also, there were people for whom and to whom I was responsible. When you know certain things about people and events and you walk away, the people you know about become very nervous. To just stop living the life would have opened me up to another shooting.

For the first time in my life, I felt a sense of fear about what I was doing. I was afraid to be on the streets. I don't know if it was because of getting shot, going to church with Broderick, or a combination of the two, but I had lost the confidence I once had in being a criminal. I now understood how other people felt when confronted with street violence.

Pursued

I must admit, however, that I wasn't completely scared straight. A few months later in the spring of 1976, I was with a friend in Modesto, California. I had a bag of heroin, and we started snorting it and drinking heavily. Even though I wanted to change, I was still being pursued by my demons. Satan had a grip on me, though it wasn't nearly as strong as it used to be.

As the night wore on, though, I slowly realized something: No matter how hard I tried, I couldn't get high. It was as if the drugs no longer had an effect on me.

The next morning, after a long night of partying, I was sitting at the kitchen table with my friend, James Hatten, whom I called "Hat." We were listening to R&B music on the radio when the station suddenly changed to gospel music.

"We need to go to church," I said.

Hat must have thought I was tripping. We didn't know anyone in Modesto and certainly didn't know anything about the churches in the area. Hat was my friend, and he knew I was trying to get away from our old life. He was tired of the junk in our lives, too. He agreed to go with me. I would do anything for Hat, I loved him that much; his agreeing to go to church was his brotherly expression of love to me.

"We'll drive down the 99 [the freeway] and stop at the first church we see," I told him.

We got dressed, jumped in my car, and headed out. A few exits down the freeway, we found Progressive Missionary Baptist Church on Fourth Street. When we walked in the doors, I felt the same peace and comfort I had experienced when the voice came to me in the hospital bed. I recognized the serenity immediately. I listened to the choir sing beautifully, then heard Reverend James Anderson's sermon. I knew this church was the place I needed to be. I couldn't wait to return the next Sunday. I felt so relieved to finally be connected to something good.

Four Sundays later, on June 13, 1976, I accepted Reverend Anderson's invitation to come to the altar and turn my life over to Jesus Christ. I joined the church and treated it as a place of accountability.

You may wonder what was different about this visit to the altar. Hadn't I accepted Christ already? Well, when I went to the altar at Galilee Missionary Baptist Church in Stockton, I knew I needed help; I was seventeen and troubled. I thought going to the altar would instantly turn me around. It didn't.

When I went to the altar at White Rose Church of God in Christ, I felt the pain of my prior life and the harm associated with my life decisions. I went to the altar and removed some of the layers of my past. My life was very conflicted. I wanted to do right, I honestly felt I was sincere in standing at the altar, but still, I had some stuff inside that was battling for space with the Holy Spirit.

When I went to Progressive Missionary Baptist Church, I entered the doors empty. Immediately, I felt the same peace I'd experienced after Jesus spoke to me on that hospital gurney. I knew that this was my chance, and if I did not make the most of the opportunity to live for Christ I would die.

After a few weeks of going to this church, as I sat and reflected on who I was and who I wanted to become, I knew that the peace that came with that voice in the hospital was the answer to the void—of abandonment, disillusionment, rejection, and abuse—I had been trying to fill for years. When I went to the altar this last time, there was no turning back. I was finally ready to rid my life of drugs, violence, and the people who were negative influences. I knew that my walk of faith with Christ was real.

Prayer

One night, while in bed with my girlfriend, I heard a voice tell me to get up and pray: "I have something for you to do." It was the same voice I'd heard while lying in the hospital bed after I was shot six times, and He was delivering the same message to me. I climbed out of bed, dropped to my knees, and asked God to reveal His plan and purpose for me. As it says in Proverbs 3:5-6, "Trust in the Lord with all your heart and lean not on your own understanding; in all your ways submit to him, and he will make your paths straight."

My girlfriend, who had witnessed much of my criminal life, woke up and asked me why I was on my knees.

"I'm praying," I said. "The Lord has called me to preach." My girlfriend did not say anything. While on my knees, I was reminded of my mission to be a chaplain. The how of the mission would take a lot longer to fulfill. However, that night I remembered that I was called to minister at San Quentin.

Well, early the next morning, my girlfriend asked me to take her home. I never saw her again. I think she believed that I was losing my mind and wanted nothing more to do with me.

Later in the week, I went to Turlock and found a guy named Randy Cloud. In 1975, I had burglarized his apartment and stolen his sound system. I knew who he was from around school. I told him that I had accepted Christ as my Savior, and that I had something for him. I don't know why I kept his stereo system, but I still had it and felt I needed to return it. When Randy saw the stuff, he started to cry. He was a Vietnam veteran and had bought the system as he prepared to return to the United States.

A few months ago, I received an e-mail from Randy talking about the impact of my returning his equipment. He said it was a true moment of challenge and change for him as well.

Angel

Shortly after I started attending Progressive Missionary Baptist Church, I met Angel Anderson, the preacher's daughter. I still remember the first time I noticed her singing in the choir. I told my friend Hat, "Wow, man, I'm going to marry her." Hat thought I was crazy. He didn't think a preacher's daughter would get involved with a street thug.

At first, Angel's parents certainly didn't want her to have anything to do with me. Her father didn't trust me and didn't think I was good enough for his daughter. I think Angel's parents figured I was only drifting. It took a long time for me to convince them that I was truly a changed man.

During one of Reverend Anderson's sermons on the second Sunday of August 1976, he shared the Bible story of Jonah, who had tried to run away from God after he was commanded to preach repentance to the city of Nineveh. The Bible tells us Jonah found God's command unbearable and tried to escape to the sea to avoid his destiny. In response, God sent a violent storm, which threatened to break Jonah's ship into pieces. Jonah was convinced that he was responsible for the storm, so he persuaded the crew to throw him overboard. When they did, the sea grew calm. The crew believed they had made a sacrifice to God.

Instead of drowning, Jonah was swallowed by a giant fish. Jonah repented and cried out to God in prayer: "But I, with shouts of grateful praise, will sacrifice to you. What I have vowed I will make good. I will say, 'Salvation comes from the Lord'" (Jonah 2:9). After three days, the fish vomited Jonah onto dry land, and he walked through Nineveh proclaiming that in forty days the city would be destroyed if the people didn't repent. Surprisingly, the people believed Jonah's message. God had compassion for them and didn't destroy Nineveh.

As I sat listening to Reverend Anderson's sermon, I was convinced he was talking about me. Tears filled my eyes. I turned to Angel, who was sitting next to me in a pew. "Why is your father talking about me?" I asked. "Why does he keep using my name? Everybody is looking at me."

Sometimes, when you hear the preached Word, everything around you seems to disappear, and you feel as though you are in a one-on-one conversation with God. As I sat with Angel, I did not know I was experiencing the conviction of the Word. What I heard was Pastor Anderson saying over and over that Earl was running from God's call to duty. The message started about Jonah but ended about me.

Of course, Reverend Anderson wasn't talking to or about me, but I felt an overwhelming guilt for ignoring God's plans. I had this experience less than a year after I was shot. Between the day God told me of my mission in October 1975, and now, in August 1976, I had not put anything into place for San Quentin. I actually did not know how to begin. I felt guilty knowing that I could have been doing more for the God who had saved my life and given me a purpose. I felt guilty because I knew there was more I could do to affect the kingdom.

I still didn't fully understand why God was talking to me. With all the harm I had inflicted on others, God shouldn't have wanted to use me to spread His message, but He did. I knew it was time for me to heed God's command.

Finally, I was beginning to believe that I was receiving the Lord's guidance and grace, despite everything I'd done. I finally knew His will, and I could no longer allow doubt, fear, or willful sin to keep me from obeying Him.

Call

After the sermon that day, I told Reverend Anderson that I had been called to preach. He asked me what I'd heard, and I told him about God saying, "You are not going to die. You have things to do. You will be a chaplain at San Quentin." I told Reverend Anderson I heard the same message again when God told me to pray.

After talking with the reverend, I went to see Reverend Dr. Henry F. Dean, who had baptized me as a child at Emmanuel Missionary Baptist Church in Stockton. I had fallen out of touch with the members of the church. My dad was still a member of its trustee board, but the church was embarrassed by my past behavior. The people there knew what I'd been doing and didn't want to be associated with me. In fact, when I was shot, Dr. Dean didn't come to the hospital to check on me; I guess he assumed that I was a lost soul.

Reverend Dean told me that if I was serious about becoming a preacher, I needed to attend Bishop, a historically black college in Dallas. The Baptist Home Mission Society founded the college in 1881 as part of a movement to educate African-American Baptists. "If you're really going to be a preacher, the only school to go to is in Dallas," Reverend Dean said.

So, I decided I would move to Texas, study religion, and become a preacher.

Ossie and Big Momma

Once I had decided that preaching was truly my calling, I went to see the two women who mattered most to me. Ossie had shown me unconditional love and Big Momma, forgiveness. They were always pulling for me and encouraging me. I wanted them to know about this change in my life.

Ossie Pittsfield, the woman who cared for me as a child and taught me how to love others, was living in a convalescent home. She had been badly injured a couple of years earlier, when a street thug stole her purse, knocked her down on a sidewalk, and broke her hip. I was never able to find out who did it. Ossie's mind was beginning to slip, and she didn't even recognize me during some of my visits. At the time, we didn't know that she was suffering from Alzheimer's disease.

I walked into Ossie's room and pulled a chair close to her bed. I grabbed her hand and said, "Grandma, I need to tell you something. You don't have to worry about me anymore. I have my life in order."

I told Ossie that I had accepted Jesus Christ as my Savior, and I was going to follow His way no matter what. Ossie looked at me with tears in her eyes. I felt that she really understood what I was saying. It was as if her mind snapped into lucidity when I told her I'd been saved.

"Oh, I've been so worried about you, baby," she told me. "There is nothing better than living for Jesus."

We talked for a little while longer about the things we used to do when I was a little boy: our visits to the train station and the wonderful meals she cooked for me. Then, her mind started drifting again. I hugged her and gave her a kiss. As I walked to my car, I couldn't stop crying. Ossie meant so much to me, and it was important to me for her to know that I was going to be okay.

A few weeks later, as I returned to my old neighborhood to visit the barbershop, my grandmother, Ella Mae Clark or "Big Momma," as our family called her, told me that Ossie had died. She was eighty-five. It hurt so bad to learn that Ossie had passed away, but I couldn't help but think she had been waiting on me to get my life in order before she joined the Lord in heaven.

I was eager to tell Big Momma what God had planned for the rest of my life as well. As her moniker might suggest, my mother's mother was a big woman. She was shorter than five feet but probably weighed more than three hundred pounds. My grandmother had a wicked backhand slap, and my siblings and I always tried to avoid it. Big Momma couldn't move very well, but she'd hit you with her big, meaty hand if you were in trouble. Despite that, I knew my grandmother loved me dearly. She took me on trips back to Texas to see her family, which got me away from my neighborhood for the summer. The display of love was not in what she did as much as in how she made me feel. And after all the mistakes I made and the disappointment I gave her, Big Momma always forgave me.

When I told Big Momma about my being called to preach, she started to cry and hugged me. We were in her kitchen and she was frying fish and cooking Chinese mustard and collard greens. She told me how proud she was of me, and that she always knew that I would be okay.

Later, when I started preaching, Big Momma took me shopping. I was wearing fly street clothes, and I'm sure I didn't look anything like a preacher. She took me to Berg's Department Store in Stockton and purchased two suits for me. I'm still not sure where she came up with the money to buy them, but she really wanted me to have them.

When I told my mother what I intended to do, she told me, "Don't play with God. He don't use people like you." My mother was being honest. I might have said the same thing to her if she had done what I'd done in the past. I was a bad person until then, but I was determined to change.

I Was a Sophomore Transfer

On January 2, 1977, my cousin Donnie Ray Chambliss and I loaded up our belongings in my 1969 Ford Fairlane and began the long drive to Dallas. Donnie, who was only a few months younger than me, had been an all-state basketball player at Franklin High School in Stockton. He attended San Joaquin Delta College, a community college, then transferred to Santa Clara University, where he continued playing basketball. Like me, Donnie was troubled and in need of direction in his life. He announced his call to preach during the summer of 1976, after dedicating his life to Jesus Christ as his Lord and Savior. He preached his first public sermon three weeks before I did.

When Donnie and I arrived in Dallas, it was snowing and the roads were covered in ice. We looked at each other and thought, *what are we doing here?* More surprises were in store. Soon after we arrived at Bishop College, we discovered a lot of the guys there were drinking and smoking weed. Many of the students were the sons of pastors from big churches. They had a lot more money than we did, since we were no longer doing anything illegal.

I'd left home so that I wouldn't do that junk anymore! I was trying to rid my life of bad influences. For much of my first semester at college, I was able to avoid falling into my past habits.

I went home to Stockton the summer after my first year at Bishop College. Things were getting pretty serious between Angel and me, and I asked her to marry me. We knew that her parents would never consent to the marriage, so we eloped to Reno, Nevada.

One week after we were married, I went back to Bishop College to resume my classes. Angel wanted to move to Dallas with me, but I told her the timing wasn't right. In all honesty, I didn't want my wife to interfere with my life choices. I knew that Angel was the best thing that had ever happened to me, but I did not know how to value who she was. I was back to being an actor. I hadn't even told my parents or siblings that I was married; only two of my closest friends, Frank Crosby and Hat, knew that we'd eloped.

Sophomore

After returning to school, I started doing what I swore I wouldn't: partying. During my second year at Bishop, I pledged a fraternity, Omega Psi Phi. Six other preachers and I started the journey, but they quit for various reasons. I knew quitting wasn't an option for me. I knew that there were some great preachers and men who were Omegas, and I was determined to join them. I believed that if I allowed my life choices to conform to the examples these men provided, perhaps I would change by virtue of close association with men of character. On December 2, 1977, I crossed the sands of Omega by myself.

Somehow, I made it through the second year of college, even though I was smoking weed and drinking again. I knew that it wasn't right. If God was testing me to see if I was okay, I failed Him miserably. Good associations didn't automatically correct my character, as I'd hoped.

Eventually, Angel became so frustrated that she sent me annulment papers, which I never signed. Every time she asked me about the papers, I told her they were in the mail. I put it off for as long as I could. I knew that Angel was a really good person, and that I was probably never going to find another woman like her. She wanted so badly to come be with me in Dallas, yet I did everything I could to keep her from being there. It was not about her; it was about me. I was immature, and I had truly done her a disservice by marrying her. She certainly deserved better. Even though I could make everything look and sound right, it was not right.

Smitty

While Angel was in California begging me to let her come and live with me, I was in Dallas living as Smitty. My house was off campus and was where most of the frat guys came by to hang out and have meetings. I finally stopped partying and had a full-time job at the Federal Reserve Bank and carried eighteen units at school. I did not have time to do much but work and study. Still, I placed too much importance on fraternity relationships and not enough on my marriage.

Well, all the issues came to a head when Charlotte, a woman with whom I had slept a couple of times, told me she was pregnant. I did not believe her. I let it pass for a few weeks, but then she became more persistent. I told her that I was married and that there was nothing I could do for her or with her. I then wrote Angel and started a trail of deceit, trying to cover up something that I could not hide—my relationship with this woman while I was married to Angel.

Shortly after Charlotte told me she was pregnant, I had to undergo surgery to remove a bullet from my face. It had been lodged there since Steven Moore shot me. Somehow, in the midst of the Omega Psi Phi pledge process, the bullet moved and was causing breathing problems. By this time, Angel had moved to Pittsburgh, because she had family support there. We were married, yet I was not ready to assume the role required for the relationship. Angel was eager to settle in and live our lives as one. She was in Pittsburgh because of my immaturity.

Upon hearing that I was going into the hospital for surgery, Angel decided it was time for her to be with me no matter what. It was true; I did need her with me. I just didn't know how to show it or respect her choice.

Angel came to Dallas and moved in with me. I realized it was time for me to settle down and become a man, but I still wasn't sure what that meant. Angel took a job working the night shift at Frito-Lay, while I worked in the mailroom and processed checks at the Federal Reserve Bank.

Things were okay, yet the pending birth of the child was hanging over me like a cloud. I finally talked with Angel about the situation but told her the child wasn't mine. At the time, I honestly didn't know if that was true or not. Angel was hurt and confused. She had been loyal to me, yet I did not return the same level of commitment. She hoped, as I did, that the baby wasn't mine.

Tiffany

On May 6, 1979, I graduated from Bishop College. It was supposed to be one of the happiest days of my life. My mom and dad came to Dallas for the ceremony. Irving, my best friend and fraternity brother, was graduating with me, and so were some of the guys who had started the pledge process with me. Many of our fraternity brothers—guys I'd pledged under and others who joined the frat after I did—showed up to give me support.

As I walked out of Carr P. Collins Chapel after receiving my degree, I was hugging Angel and talking with my friends. When I looked up, I realized that my mother and Charlotte were standing together right in front of me. They were hugging and making quite a show. It was strange to me because the girl wasn't graduating. I guess she was there to support some of her sorority sisters and to meet my mother.

I was upset, and I realized it was the perfect situation for my mother. It was another reason for her to say, "God don't use people like you." My mother knew that I was married, but she did not like Angel. Angel made me happy, and my mother could not deal with that. When Charlotte brought my mother into this situation, my mother enjoyed it.

On September 23, 1979, two years after Angel and I were married, Tiffany was born. With the involvement of my mother with Charlotte, a close relationship with Tiffany was doomed from the start. I chose not to involve myself in any dealings with my mother. She assisted Charlotte in coming to California and getting her child support payments raised based on state law. My mother seemed to enjoy playing emotional games and trying to hurt Angel, which was the next best thing if she could not get directly at me. The choice I made was one to keep my marriage intact and have a family with Angel. Thankfully, Angel was strong and loved me enough to forgive my mistakes.

Despite my absence, Tiffany has done well for herself. In 2013, she finished college with a teaching degree. My sister Betty Jo and I flew to Texas for her graduation ceremony. In hindsight, I wish I'd been more involved in Tiffany's life, but circumstances never allowed it. On occasion I visited Dallas and saw Tiffany. When she was eighteen, I sat down and explained my life choices to her. I admitted that I had been a father to her, but had not been a dad to her. Her birth certificate had my name listed as father, I did not do the things necessary to be called her dad.

We talk on occasion, but I cannot say that I have the same kind of relationship with Tiffany that I have with my other children. I just didn't do a good job. Tiffany has become who she is in spite of my failure. If I had a chance to do it over again, from the point of conception I would have been much more honest with Angel, which would have set a different course for how I dealt with Tiffany. Yet, I also knew that as long as my mother was associated with Tiffany's mother, I was not going to become involved with them. Sadly, my feelings for my mother leaked in and corrupted my relationship with Tiffany and her mother.

The Scouts

After I graduated from Bishop College, my counselors told me that, with my criminal background, my career objective of becoming a prison chaplain was probably unrealistic. I'd never been charged with a serious crime, but my past as a drug dealer would probably prevent me from getting a job in a prison. I was advised to take a job with the Boy Scouts of America, an organization that I was a part of as a kid.

I knew the job would be very rewarding and would give me a chance to make a positive impact on kids. I took a job with the Circle Ten Council in Dallas, then was transferred to the San Francisco Bay Area Council as a scout executive. Eventually, I became the first person in the Western Region to be named a senior district scout executive. It was a chance for Angel and me to return home to California. We lived with my godmother until we were able to find an apartment in Daly City. We settled down into the life of a married couple and our relationship grew stronger over time.

In the back of my mind, though, I knew that I would one day be working behind the bars of San Quentin Prison, regardless of what anyone said. Fulfilling God's word to me became my mission in life. I knew that God's grace was sufficient to get me beyond any circumstance, enough to supply everything I needed. Deep inside, I knew I'd be contradicting what God said if I settled for any position other than that of chaplain at San Quentin. It was what I was called to do, in the most dramatic and life-changing fashion possible.

$\underline{5}$

Cell 66

Wᴴɪʟᴇ I ᴡᴀs ᴡᴏʀᴋɪɴɢ ғᴏʀ the Boy Scouts of America in San Francisco, I was introduced to Buzz Brewer, a major in the Salvation Army, at a Kiwanis International meeting. A few weeks later, Brewer saw me again at another meeting. "Hey, didn't you say you wanted to be a prison chaplain?" he asked.

"Yes, sir."

"Well, there's an opening at San Quentin," he said. "They already have a pretty good idea of who they're going to hire, but you should apply anyway. It would be a good way to get your foot in the door."

I was so busy with what I was doing for the Boy Scouts—and Angel and I had a growing family at home—that I didn't apply for the job. A few weeks later, Buzz saw me again and asked about it. I told him I hadn't applied, figuring that I wouldn't waste my time if they already knew whom they wanted to hire.

"I didn't think you would," he said. "Here's the application. Fill it out and send it in."At Buzz's urging, I filled out the State of California employment application and mailed it. A few weeks later, I received a response letter, telling me I didn't meet the minimum qualifications for the prison position. I balled up the letter and threw it in a trashcan, believing my dream of becoming San Quentin's chaplain was over. But then, a voice told me, "Call and ask them what you need to do." I retrieved the letter and called the phone number listed on the stationery.

When I reached a woman with the state's personnel department, she told me they'd mistakenly sent me the wrong letter. She told me that I was actually qualified for the position and that they would send another letter. She said I was welcome to go to Napa State Hospital for a job interview.

I was surprised, given my criminal past. However, the reality was that I did not have an adult arrest record. I was the victim when I was shot. So, I was officially qualified to work at the prison.

When I went to the hospital for my interview, an ex-con who had already been promised the job was sitting in the waiting area. "You can go back home," he told me.

"It's okay," I said. "I need the interviewing experience anyway."

San Quentin Prison officials did end up hiring the ex-con for the job, but I thought my interview went very well. The man that they hired had been paroled from the California prison system and had gone back to college to get his degree. He was a perfect example of the possibility of change for inmates. At least now, prison officials could put a face with my name, and it was a good experience to interview and meet with them.

Hired

Five months later, San Quentin Prison officials let the man go before his probationary period ended. San Quentin wasn't the right fit for him, and he's doing great work at another correctional facility. They sent me a letter and then called, asking me to come back to San Quentin to interview for the Protestant chaplain position. Lee Cribb, the chief deputy warden, conducted my interview. He was twice called away during my interview because of inmates' deaths. I also met Chaplain Harry Howard, who would become my mentor and was the best prison chaplain I ever met. I remember Harry saying, "You're twenty-seven, the same age as my son. How have you done so much already?" He was referring to my educational training and community work with the Boy Scouts and the church. I told him I was not in a position to compare myself to his son (or anyone else).

I was hired by the State of California and given my assignment. On July 15, 1983, I walked through the iron gates of San Quentin to begin serving what would be a twenty-three-year tenure as the prison chaplain. At the time, I was the youngest person ever hired for that position in the state of California. It was a fulfillment of my promise to God, who saved me as I lay bleeding in a hospital bed, and to my father, who had seen God's hand in my life even when I couldn't. The most harrowing, spiritually challenging, and rewarding period of my life was about to begin.

When I first walked past the granite walls of San Quentin, I had no idea what I was really getting myself into. I knew of San Quentin's reputation as one of the most dangerous places in the world. Americans have long been fascinated by what happens inside its walls. The prison was built in 1852 on a point of land that juts into San Francisco Bay. Inmates provided the construction labor; they slept on the prison ship *Waban* at night and labored to build the new institution during the day. The rudimentary prison, which included a dungeon and a whipping post, became home to some of the most notorious cutthroats and swindlers drawn to San Francisco during the great Gold Rush.

In 1891, Folsom and San Quentin prisons were officially declared the state's designated execution sites. The first hanging at San Quentin occurred in 1893. More than two hundred people were hanged there before 1937, when the state legislature replaced the noose with lethal gas as the official method of execution. San Quentin housed both male and female inmates until 1933, when the women's prison at Tehachapi was built. Today, San Quentin sits on 432 acres overlooking the bay, only twelve miles north of the Golden Gate Bridge. It is located in Marin County, one of the wealthiest in the country.[1] A 2001 study estimated the waterfront land might be worth more than $600 million.[2] But many of the men who live there are broke—mentally and spiritually.

Inmates

The walled prison consists of four large cell blocks identified by their cardinal directions: West, South, North, and East, as well as one maximum-security cell block aptly named the Adjustment

Center. There are also a central health care services building, a medium-security dorm setting, and a minimum-security firehouse. At various times, San Quentin has been home to more than seven hundred condemned inmates, making its death row the most populated in the country.

Amazingly, I was only beginning to learn my way around the prison when God decided to test me mightily. It was Tuesday, December 13, 1983, fewer than five months after I had started working at San Quentin. I was still getting to know the inmates and they were becoming more familiar with me. A couple of weeks before Christmas, I was distributing holiday cards that the inmates could fill out and send to loved ones. As I worked my way through the various sections of the prison, I was finding the task to be one of my more pleasant duties. Even inside the rugged walls of San Quentin, the inmates were in a holiday spirit and liked having something to look forward to.

I was one of three Protestant chaplains working at San Quentin, and my areas of assignment included the Adjustment Center, Alpine Section, North Block, as well as an area dubbed "Tent City." North Block had two sides, each being five tiers high. One side housed rank-and-file gang members, while the other side was home to maximum-security inmates—the truly violent and rebellious men who couldn't be trusted in the general population. The gang side of North Block was segregated by race and gang affiliation. Members of the Black Guerilla Family—a prison and street gang founded in 1966 by George Jackson and W. L. Nolen while they were incarcerated—lived on one tier, the Aryan Brotherhood on another, and the Mexican Mafia on another. Members of the Bloods and Crips were also separated.

The Adjustment Center was the prison within the prison. It was home to the worst inmates, and it was the place no one wanted to go. It was three levels of six-by-eight cells that largely housed high-ranking gang members, violent offenders, and condemned prisoners. Many of the men in the Adjustment Center were isolated because it was believed that they were capable of ordering executions from behind bars.

Connection

My job that afternoon was to deliver bundles of five to ten Christmas cards to about five hundred inmates along with my holiday wishes. I had volunteers who would have gladly completed the task for me, but it was really my opportunity to get to know the guys personally. More than anything, I wanted to learn as much as I could about the inmates as individuals, then develop ways to bridge the gap between them and me and, more important, between them and the Lord.

Since I had been working at San Quentin for only a few months, I'd had very limited contact with most of the inmates. However, I knew a few better than others because I'd grown up with them on the streets. In fact, I was familiar with a few of the members of the Black Guerilla Family. I didn't know any of them were serving time at San Quentin until I arrived there. I didn't go out of my way to track down the Black Guerilla Family members I knew from my past; I was trying to put my former life in the rearview mirror as much as possible. Since I was still working in a probationary period, I didn't want to give my superiors any reason to let me go. I was a prison chaplain; I knew that I had to be above reproach.

On that day, I delivered the first batch of one hundred cards to the inmates in the Adjustment Center, which was right across from the prison chapel. I greeted each inmate the same way: "Merry Christmas." I spent a little extra time with One-Eyed Mike, a leader of the Aryan Brotherhood. For some reason, we had connected and I enjoyed talking to him about his past life as a chaplain's clerk and some of the things he did to wind up in the Adjustment Center.

I was surprised that nearly every one of them offered me the same response: "Thank you. Merry Christmas to you." It gave me reassurance that I might actually be able to connect with some of the most hardened men.

Shooter

I finished giving out cards in the Adjustment Center and pulled my cart to North Block. Slowly I worked my way along the second tier of the North Block, where the Black Guerilla Family members were housed, then up to tiers four (Aryan Brotherhood) and five (Mexican Mafia). Then I got more cards and headed back out for my appointed rounds.

When you first come to the prison and introduce yourself to the inmates, they ask you a battery of questions to make sure you're not a so-called rat for the warden, someone trying to obtain information about gang operations. During my first few weeks on the job, many of the inmates quizzed me, especially because I was an

African-American chaplain. They asked me, "Where are you from?" "Who did you know there?" "What neighborhood did you run in?"

Early in my ministry at San Quentin, one such encounter helped me earn the trust of many of the inmates. As I made my way through the prison one evening, I arrived at one cell that was pitch black. I heard a voice from the darkness, but I could see only his silhouette.

"You from Stockton?" he asked.

"Yes," I said. "You know I'm from Stockton." I'd learned to keep my responses brief, because some inmates will attempt to get you to reveal personal information so they can threaten your family.

"Man, you ain't from Stockton," he said.

"I'm from the east side," I said. "I don't have time for games. What do you need?"

The inmate started laughing, and then turned the light on. It was one of my old friends. He yelled out something in Swahili and all the guys on the tier started laughing. It turned out that he was one of the leaders on the tier, and his approval sealed the deal that I was okay.

Now, as I continued passing out the Christmas cards, eventually making my way around to the Adjustment Center side of North Block to Cell Two North 65 and then 66, I had no idea whom I would encounter next. The man in Cell 66 was leaning against the door, gripping the bars. When I looked at him to hand him his bundle of cards, I felt my stomach drop. A wave of nausea struck me. I broke out in a cold sweat. He looked at me quizzically, not recognizing me yet.

"What's your name?" I asked. His eyes widened and I could see panic on his face as he recognized me. He jumped away from the bars, placing his back against the wall of his cell.

"Ace," he said. Then he cried, "I got shot, too! I got shot, too, man!"

"Ace" was actually Steven Moore, the guy who shot me six times and tried to kill me in my apartment on October 22, 1975. He had been only seventeen years old at the time, a member of the Insane Crips gang. He had been visiting family in Stockton and met Michael, one of my drug dealers. Michael persuaded Steven to come to my apartment and kill me. Ace received a slap on the wrist for nearly killing me; he was doing time at San Quentin for drug-related charges. Even though I'd seen him at court during his criminal trial for shooting me, it was the first time I'd had a chance to confront him.

At that moment, I realized that while eight years had passed and I had gone to school and preached (I had been the youth pastor at Olivet Baptist Church in San Francisco while I worked for the Boy Scouts of America) and started a ministry, I had never truly forgiven my shooter. In college, I learned to understand the theory behind forgiveness. However, the idea of forgiveness is a bunch of nonsense until you're confronted with that one overwhelming, negative thing. Since I hadn't forgiven Steven for what he'd done to me, I hadn't yet healed from the episode, either. I knew since God had forgiven me for my past transgressions, I needed to forgive Steven. As it says in Matthew 6:14-15, "For if you forgive men when they sin against you, your heavenly Father will also forgive you. But if you do not forgive men their sins, your Father will not forgive your sins."

As I stood staring at the man who had nearly ended my life, I tried to muster the courage and strength to forgive him. My heart was racing; my blood pressure was probably off the charts. I was sweating profusely and a million thoughts were going through my head. In the back of my mind, I knew Steven deserved to die for what he had done to me. At the moment, I wanted him dead. Yet, as a Christian, I knew I had to forgive him. I didn't know what to do next.

Dilemma

I slid a stack of Christmas cards between the bars. Ace slowly approached me, as though he feared that at any moment I would brandish a concealed firearm and gun him down. He took the cards that I set on his bars, and I walked away to the next cell. As I did, I started to weep.

At the time, I knew it would have been easy for me to get someone to kill Ace. I could have taken him out eight years earlier, when my buddies came to my parents' home wanting to kill him. I had declined the opportunity then, but now I was presented with a second opportunity to avenge what he'd done to me. I could have mentioned to one of my friends that he was the guy who shot me and, without my asking, my friend would kill Steven, and the act would never have been traced back to me. I knew that was the way it worked in San Quentin.

In my heart, I knew I couldn't do it. It would have been a betrayal of everything I was supposed to stand for now and what I had become. If Steven was killed because of me or if I'd asked someone to kill Steven, I would have betrayed God, my father, and myself.

As I continued to walk from cell to cell, tears were streaming down my face. I could no longer find the strength to say "Merry Christmas" to the inmates. Many of them saw me and became concerned.

"What's wrong, Chap?" asked one.

"Hey, guys, something's wrong with Smithy!" one of them yelled.

I couldn't answer. My head was pounding with suppressed anger. Somehow, I made it all the way to cell 100 at the end of the tier, but the only way off the tier took me back past Cell 66—and Steven Moore. I dreaded walking by his cell again. What would I say to him? What would I do to him?

I had no choice, so I turned around and started to make the long walk back. "You okay, Chap?" one inmate asked. I didn't respond. My body was clammy with perspiration. It took everything I had to keep putting one foot in front of the other. I arrived at Ace's cell. He was standing with his back to the wall, hands behind his back, with a frightened look in his eyes. Part of me wanted to say something to terrorize him—to make him think I was going to have him killed. Then, abruptly, I knew what I had to say.

"Hey, I want to thank you for shooting me," I said too softly for anyone but Ace to hear. "God used you to get to me."

They were the hardest words I had ever spoken. As soon as I said them, however, I felt as though I'd been released. Suddenly, I didn't feel any animosity toward Steven Moore.

Ace just stared at me. It was obvious he didn't know what to say. I went back to my office, retrieved more bundles of Christmas cards, and passed them out to the inmates on the rest of my cell-blocks. Once I was finished, I went back to my office, sat down, and started sobbing. Until that moment, I hadn't known how much pain I'd been carrying—and how many people I'd hurt carrying that pain and pretending I wasn't.

I didn't tell anyone who worked at the prison about my encounter with Ace. Ace wrote a letter to the warden. My supervisor, associate warden George Jackson, called me to his office and showed me Steven's letter. He said, "This is from an inmate who says he shot you, and he thinks you are going to have him killed." I was sure Jackson would fire me immediately because of my history with an inmate. I told him the safest place in the world for Moore to be was at San Quentin. I told Jackson I had forgiven Ace, and I believe that he sensed that I was sincere.

Right before Christmas, Jackson transferred Ace to another prison. The easiest thing for him to do would have been to let me go. If I hadn't stopped and said what I did to Ace, I don't think I would have had the peace I had when Jackson confronted me.

It is now clear to me why God made sure that I would confront Ace. He wanted me to discover how to show the same kind of grace and forgiveness that He had shown me years earlier. He wanted me to teach the inmates how to forgive and ask for forgiveness. It was a lesson that I would never forget during my twenty-three-year tenure at the Bastille by the Bay.

6

Geronimo and Huey

My first few months working as the chaplain at San Quentin Prison were eye opening. At lunch, during my first day of orientation, I asked if I could walk around the prison. I still remember hearing for the first time the sounds of prison gates and cell doors being slammed shut. They are sounds you never forget. Hearing them reaffirmed what I already knew: Once you were inside San Quentin, you weren't leaving until the court system let you go.

During my initial tour, I met some of the inmates who were assigned to work in the chapel. When one of them told me that he didn't think Christians should smoke, I threw away the packet of cigarettes in my pocket and never smoked again.

I noticed very early that there weren't a lot of people walking around the upper and lower yards of the prison. Someone always seemed to be getting shanked with a homemade knife, which would throw the prison into lockdown twenty-four hours a day. In fact, San Quentin was on lockdown during thirteen of my first sixteen months on the job.

Walking around the prison for the first time, I met one of the only white guys from my old Stockton neighborhood, Bobby, who told me he'd started a so-called church, Satan's Chosen. In speaking to Bobby, I could tell that he wasn't the same person I'd known on the outside. Being in prison had truly changed him, for the worse. When I went home after my first day on the job, the enormity of what I'd taken on stunned me.

Getting the inmates to trust and interact with me was a continuous challenge. In the first few months, only a handful of inmates seemed interested in my ministry and attended my chapel services. Eventually, I figured out that spending time with the inmates, by playing chess or dominoes with them, was the easiest way to get to know them. On many days, I'd ask the guards to allow me to keep eight to ten guys in the chapel on out count when they were supposed to be in their housing units for the four o'clock count. I'd send volunteers to get burgers and French fries, and then we'd get all of the guys together and work with them as a group. I knew my mission was twofold: to be an example of the Bible to them and to be somebody they wanted to be around.

Group

Eventually, I started working with six or seven inmates more closely than the others, and they became the first ushers at my chapel. I knew they were at the top of the food chain in their prison groups, and I needed their endorsements to get the rest of the prison population to buy into what I was trying to do. They were hardened men with violent backgrounds, but they were interesting characters and worked together in helping me bring more men to the Lord.

Ramon Renteria was one of the inmates in the Southern Mexican Car. Bruce White, who had been a major drug dealer in San Francisco and was serving a life sentence for killing one of his runners, was heavily involved in the 415, a gang started by inmates from the Bay Area. Inmates from Oakland and San Francisco formed the gang as an answer to the Southern California gangs.

Russell Coleman was the youngster, not a leader, but he knew who was who among the younger inmates. He was a kid from Long Beach, California, and a member of the Crips. He couldn't read and wasn't educated, but he was street smart, and the other prisoners in my group made him learn to read and write and work toward getting a GED in order for him to hang with them. It was rewarding to see the older inmates caring for a younger guy.

Lionel "Pete" McCoy had beaten a murder rap in San Francisco when a judge declared a mistrial, but he was arrested again for kidnapping and was serving a life sentence. Pete was a clerk at the Captain's Porch, where all of the daily paperwork was processed and the facility captain maintained his office. Pete seemed to know everyone in the prison and how to get things done.

Joe Broughton had two nicknames: "Slow Joe" and "Bloody

Joe." Joe talked really slow, but the other inmates knew he was capable of killing them at the drop of a hat. Jimmy Reese ("JR") and Gypsy Sheets, who were both serving life sentences for murder, were also part of my group.

Banquet

The semi-lockdowns ended and, after several months of meeting with the guys, I told them, "I have a plan. If we can have a truce where nobody gets stabbed or killed for a couple of months, we're going to have a big banquet. You can each invite your people and every convict can invite two people from the outside. We'll have a chapel service and then we'll have a special meal at the dining hall. Before the banquet, you can put a list together and order anything you want for your own special meal."

The guys talked with their groups about my idea, and everyone agreed there wouldn't be any stabbing or killing at San Quentin. A truce was established for a couple of months. Much to my surprise, they held up their end of the bargain. I told my ushers to get me a list of everyone who wanted to come to the banquet. On the day of the event, we had about two hundred people in the chapel. Some officers agreed to help me host.

Warden Daniel Vasquez took a big risk allowing the banquet to take place and allowing the inmates' family members to come inside the walls. But he also wanted to see a change in the prison.

Everyone had a great time, and many of the inmates asked me when we were going to do it again. As you can imagine, news spreads around the prison like wildfire, and other inmates started hearing about what was happening at the chapel. Within three months, I had a packed chapel service.

One of the rules at San Quentin was that you couldn't run across the upper prison yard. If a prison guard on one of the gun towers saw an inmate running, he would probably shoot, because he figured the prisoner was on his way to harm someone. Well, after a few months of my chapel service, the inmates knew if they showed up late, they were going to have to listen to the Word while standing—no seats would be available. Inmates started running across the yard to make sure they had a seat in the pews, and the guards gave up on the idea of trying to stop them once they reached the check-in station at four post. It was great to see the inmates so excited about coming to chapel.

Pratt

Hosting dominoes games in my office helped me interact with the prisoners individually. Among the inmates who weren't initially invited to my office was Geronimo Pratt, a high-ranking official in the Black Panther Party in the 1960s. I didn't ask him because the guys in the group said Geronimo would not want to hang around with the chaplain.

Born in Morgan City, Louisiana, Pratt was a former high-school quarterback who'd served two tours of combat in Vietnam. He reached the rank of sergeant and was awarded two Purple Hearts for his service. After Pratt was discharged from the U.S. Army, he moved to Los Angeles and started studying political science at UCLA using the G.I. Bill.

Before too long, Al "Bunchy" Carter and John Huggins re-cruited Pratt to join the Black Panther Party, which was involved in the Black Power Movement and American politics during the 1960s and 1970s. Because of his military background, Pratt rose in the Black Panther ranks quickly. He became the minister of de-fense, then chief of the L.A. Panther group after Carter and Hug-gins were gunned down in a dispute with a rival black-nationalist group on the UCLA campus. Pratt taught Black Panther recruits self-defense and weaponry.

In 1971, Pratt's wife, Saundra, was murdered; her body was found in a ditch. She had been eight months pregnant. Pratt blamed his wife's murder on a growing dispute between followers of Black Panther Party co-founder Huey Newton and popular leader Eldridge Cleaver. Pratt and his wife had supported Cleaver, and Pratt was convinced that Newton's supporters had something to do with Saundra's death.

In 1972, Pratt was convicted of murdering Caroline Olsen, a white twenty-seven-year-old elementary school teacher, who had been killed four years earlier during a robbery at a tennis court in Santa Monica, California. On the evening of December 18, 1968, Olsen and her husband were playing tennis when two black men confronted them. They took eighteen dollars from Olsen's purse. "This ain't enough," one of them told her. They ordered the couple to "lie down and pray," her husband, Kenneth Olsen, told a jury.[1] Kenneth Olsen was shot five times but survived. Caroline Olsen was shot twice and died eleven days later.

Police said the pistol fired in the shooting and the red-and-white GTO convertible used as a getaway car belonged to Pratt. Kenneth Olsen identified Pratt as the man who killed his wife. The most damaging testimony came from Julius Butler, a former Black Panther and police informant, who said Pratt boasted to him about killing the woman.

Pratt's attorney, Johnnie Cochran, who would earn worldwide fame more than thirty years later while defending former NFL running back O. J. Simpson against charges that he murdered his ex-wife and her friend, argued that Pratt was 350 miles away at the time of Olsen's death. Cochran said Pratt was in the Bay Area visiting Black Panther Party offices on the day Olsen was killed.

Nonetheless, a jury convicted Pratt of Caroline Olsen's murder on July 28, 1972. He was sentenced to life in prison and shipped to San Quentin Prison a month later. Pratt's supporters argued that his conviction was part of law enforcement's war on the Black Panther Party, which FBI director J. Edgar Hoover in September 1968 had called the greatest threat to the internal security of the country.[2]

Rebel

At San Quentin Prison, Pratt was considered a rebel, and none of the other prison chaplains wanted anything to do with him. Through a strange twist, my son Earl Jr., and his son, Hiroji, played basketball together in Marin County. I got to know Pratt when I coached the inmate football team and started to talk to a lot of guys on the exercise yard with whom I did not interact through the chapel. Some of Pratt's associates spent time with me, even though he pledged never to set foot in any chapel.

Initially, Pratt avoided me. But he started to come around once the guys convinced him I was simply trying to help, that I was not a threat to any particular structure or group. Maybe it was the food that I brought over from the staff lounge. Before long, we started playing dominoes together. After I was able to obtain a saxophone for Bruce White, Pratt told me he was a trumpet player. I was able to find Pratt an old trumpet to play, after which I could hardly get him to leave my office. It wasn't long before I learned that Pratt had confided in others that he was going to kill Newton if he ever saw him again. Pratt believed one of the reasons he was convicted was because Newton wouldn't allow any Black Panther Party members to testify on his behalf during his trial.

Like Pratt, Newton was born in Louisiana and grew up in the segregated South. He was the youngest of seven children, and his father was a sharecropper and Baptist preacher. In 1945, Newton's family moved to Oakland, where he graduated from Oakland Technical High School, even though he was illiterate. He later taught himself to read and write and attended Merritt College in Oakland and the University of California, Santa Cruz.

In October 1966, Newton and Bobby Seale formed the Black Panthers, with Seale becoming the group's chairman and Newton the minister of defense. In many ways, Newton became the iconic symbol of the Black Panther Party, brandishing weapons, wearing a black beret and leather jacket, and clenching his fist in the Black Power salute. The Black Panthers were perhaps best known for their clashes with police and protests during the turbulent 1960s. However, the group also did a lot of good work in impoverished black neighborhoods, providing many needy people with free meals and health care.

The Black Panthers were a big target for the FBI and local law enforcement, and Newton and Pratt were at the top of the list of people authorities wanted to neutralize. In 1967, Newton was charged with murdering an Oakland police officer after a shootout with police. A jury convicted him of voluntary manslaughter, but the verdict was overturned by a state Court of Appeal on grounds that the jury was not properly instructed. After two mistrials, the charges were dropped altogether. In 1974, Newton was charged with pistol-whipping his tailor and murdering a seventeen-year-old prostitute. Newton fled to Cuba, where he spent three years before returning to face the charges. The charges were dropped after juries in the cases were deadlocked; he was found guilty of being a felon in possession of a handgun.

Encounter

In August 1988, Newton arrived at San Quentin Prison to serve a short sentence for a parole violation. On the day Huey started serving his time, the officers released him in the yard, which was unheard of in the prison. Under normal protocol, new arrivals had to travel from the receiving and release area to the Reception Center. The guards, in my opinion, were essentially giving Pratt an opportunity to kill him. I do not know if that was their motive, but it's what I suspected, based on prison politics.

When Pratt saw Newton and started walking toward him, I heard later that all the prisoners on the yard held their breath because they knew what was going to happen next—or at least thought they did. Pratt approached Newton, who was terrified, and reached out and hugged his former mentor. He saw that Newton's clothes were tattered, and took Newton to get some clean clothes, then brought him to me.

It was a Thursday, and I was in my office with Bishop Donald Green who, despite his busy schedule as a pastor at a church with one of the largest congregations in San Francisco, had a weekly ministry at San Quentin. There was a knock on my door and, as I opened it, I saw Geronimo and another inmate. "Earl, this is Huey Newton," Pratt said. "He needs you." Geronimo turned around and walked back to the yard.

Newton had long struggled with addictions to alcohol and cocaine. The Huey Newton I saw did not resemble the man I had grown up wanting to emulate. In my youth, Huey represented power and force. Huey was a voice for many people who were afraid to speak about the injustices taking place. Huey seemed fearless. However, now he was broken and tired. We discussed his family, his life, and his need for salvation. With the assistance of Bishop Green, Newton accepted Jesus Christ as his Lord and Savior right there in my office. He dropped to his knees and wept like a baby, as he asked Jesus to forgive him.

After that incident, Newton and Pratt were changed men. When Pratt first saw Newton in the prison yard, he realized Newton was a different man. At that moment, Pratt figured out that holding onto his anger was keeping him captive more than San Quentin's walls and bars. Pratt told me many years later that forgiving Newton was the turning point in his life.

Huey and Geronimo buried past differences, feuds, and betrayals and became close friends again. Newton told Pratt that he had nothing to do with his wife's murder. Years later, Pratt learned that Newton had told him the truth about his wife.

When Newton was about to be released from San Quentin in February 1989, he told prison officials he wouldn't leave without Pratt. Geronimo had recently been denied parole. During the hearing, a state parole official said he was dangerous. Newton eventually left San Quentin, then was killed while leaving an Oakland crack house in a drug-infested neighborhood, on August 22, 1989. Police said a twenty-five-year-old man shot Newton because he'd stolen drugs from his gang.

Overturned

In 1997, California Superior Court Judge Everett W. Dickey vacated Pratt's conviction of killing Olsen on the grounds that Julius Butler had lied about being a government informant during his trial, and that key evidence had been withheld from Pratt's defense. Pratt had spent twenty-seven years in prison, including eight years in solitary confinement. The California Parole Board denied Pratt freedom sixteen times even as Amnesty International, the American Civil Liberties Union, and the National Association for the Advancement of Colored People fought for his release. Other supporters drew attention to his case by hanging a banner from the Statue of Liberty. For nearly three decades, Pratt argued that he'd been framed, but authorities wouldn't listen.

Americans eventually learned that the FBI had, in fact, framed him. According to the memoirs of former FBI agent Wesley Swearingen, the FBI had a wiretap at the Black Panther Party headquarters in Los Angeles at the time Olsen was killed. Wiretap logs, which proved that Pratt was in San Francisco on the day she was killed, were destroyed. Another wiretap at the Black Panther Party offices in San Francisco proved Pratt was in the Bay Area, but the evidence was withheld from his defense team.[3]

The judge also noted that Olsen's husband initially identified another man as her killer, but the jury was never informed of the evidence. The judge said Butler also lied to the jury about being a police informant. A juror in Pratt's original trial, Jeanne Rook Hamilton, told the *New York Times*: "If we had known about Butler's background, there's no way Pratt would have been convicted."[4]

Reward

The state of California lost an appeal to nullify Dickey's decision, and Pratt was awarded $4.5 million from federal and local governments as a settlement for his wrongful imprisonment. He spent some of the money trying to free Black Panther Party members who had wrongly been accused and convicted of crimes. Geronimo died on June 2, 2011, while living in a village in Tanzania. He was with a group of former black revolutionaries who taught school and helped the community. He was sixty-three.

Even faced with one of the worst injustices in American history, Pratt found the courage and strength to forgive the man that he believed helped to frame him. Some years after his release, while in New Orleans for a San Francisco 49ers' game against the New Orleans Saints, I went to dinner at former Black Panther Bruce White's house and he invited Geronimo to join us. Geronimo, Bruce, and I talked about the day that he brought Huey to the chapel. Geronimo said, "I knew what everyone expected me to do and I knew what I planned to do. But when I saw [Newton], I felt sorry for him."

I taught the inmates that nearly everyone has been hurt by someone's actions or words during his or her life; but if we don't practice forgiveness, we might be the ones who end up paying dearly. Forgiveness is making a decision to let go of our resentment and thoughts of revenge. The acts or words that hurt or offended us might always be a part of us, but forgiveness can lessen its grip and help us focus on the more positive parts of our lives. Forgiveness can even lead us to feelings of compassion and understanding for the ones who wronged us.

Geronimo learned that revenge wouldn't work. Forgiveness is a state of grace, nothing you can force or pretend. On the prison yard of San Quentin Prison, perhaps the most unlikely of places, Geronimo found the inner strength to forgive his enemy.

7

Robert Alton Harris

W HEN I INTERVIEWED TO BECOME the chaplain at San Quentin Prison for the first time, the warden asked how I would manage executions. I chuckled, feigning confidence. "No problem, I'll be able to handle it," I said.

To be honest, I didn't give much thought to how I'd handle an execution, because one hadn't happened in so long—none in California since 1967. During the Wild West days, county sheriffs were allowed to carry out executions at town-square gallows. In 1872, capital punishment was authorized in California's penal code, then the state declared in 1891 that executions could take place only at state prisons. On March 3, 1893, Jose Gabriel, a Native American, who murdered a farming couple in San Diego County, California, was the first man hanged at San Quentin. The first hanging at Folsom State Prison occurred two years later.

In August 1937, the gas chamber replaced hanging as the method of execution. The law didn't affect inmates who had already been sentenced to die, so hangings continued for the next five years. In all, 215 inmates were hanged at San Quentin.

The state's only gas chamber was built at San Quentin, and Robert Lee Cannon and Albert Kessel were the first inmates to die inside it on December 2, 1938. The two men were survivors of a bloody prison riot at Folsom, which left Warden Clarence Larkin, a prison guard, and two inmates dead. It took Cannon about twelve minutes to die in the pale green gas chamber; Kessel held on for about fifteen-and-a-half minutes. Kessel seemed to hold his breath, then gasped: "It's bad!" Spectators were so disturbed by what they saw that there was an immediate movement to repeal the new law and reinstate hanging as the state's method of execution.[1]

However, San Quentin's gas chamber survived and over the next three decades, 194 inmates were executed in it, including four women. Aaron Mitchell, who was found guilty of killing a police officer in Sacramento, California, died in the gas chamber on April 8, 1967. Several hours before Mitchell was scheduled to die, he was allowed to walk outside his cell. According to the *Los Angeles Times*, he slashed his arm with a jagged piece of metal from his headphones, and then started shouting: "I am the second coming of Jesus! I am the son of God." After a prison doctor bandaged Mitchell's arm, he picked at his cuts, smeared blood on his palms, and then stood in the crucifix position. Reverend Byron Eshelman, the prison chaplain at the time, told the newspaper that Mitchell chanted: "This is the blood of Jesus Christ . . . and I am going to save the world." Prison psychiatrists evaluated Mitchell and said he was faking his bizarre behavior to delay his death. After Mitchell was finally strapped into the execution chair, his final words were: "I am Jesus Christ!"[2]

Following Mitchell's death, there were no executions in California for the next twenty-five years because of various state and U.S. Supreme Court decisions. On February 18, 1972, the California Supreme Court declared the death penalty cruel and unusual punishment in violation of the state constitution. As a result, 107 inmates were taken off Death Row and resentenced. Four years later, after a similar California Supreme Court ruling, seventy inmates had their sentences changed to something other than death. The California State Legislature reenacted the death penalty in 1977, and then the state's voters passed Proposition 7 in 1978, which is the statute under which the death sentence operates today.[3]

Convicted

Although the death penalty was reinstated, no executions were carried out in California until April 1992, nearly nine years after I first walked through the prison gates as chaplain. The man to be executed was Robert Alton Harris, who had been sentenced to die for killing two teenage boys in San Diego. According to police, Harris and his brother Daniel abducted the two boys from a fast-food restaurant on July 5, 1978, and made them drive to an isolated area. After Robert shot and killed the sixteen-year-old boys, John Mayeski and Michael Baker, he calmly ate the hamburgers they'd purchased for lunch. Robert and Daniel drove home and used the stolen car to rob a bank, which netted them two thousand dollars. A witness from the bank robbery followed them home and called police.

Authorities apprehended Robert and Daniel and searched their home. Police found unfired rounds of ammunition on Robert, and clothing matching the description of what the bank robbers were wearing was burning in the fireplace. Police questioned Daniel Harris that evening, and he gave them a voluntary statement detailing the abduction and murder of the boys. Robert admitted robbing the bank but denied killing the teenagers. On March 6, 1979, Robert was convicted of two counts of murder in the first degree with special circumstances, as well as kidnapping, and was sentenced to death. His brother, who had cooperated with police, was convicted of kidnapping and sentenced to six years in state prison.

Robert Harris spent more than thirteen years on Death Row.

Making Up the Ministry

I could write an entire book about ministering to Death Row. For obvious reasons, few places need ministry more. The public has no idea what condemned men and women face each day. When I first started working at San Quentin, Chaplain Harry Howard was doing the ministry on a section of Condemned Row. There were ninety-plus guys when I started and the population grew rapidly. Chaplain Howard and I split Condemned Row duties.

After some months of ministry, I met Benny Hardister, a businessman from Sonoma, California, who told me he was going to halt his prison ministry: "I'm out of here. This is not working."

He'd found that moving around too much, not taking time to get to know the men was ineffective. Some time later, however, Benny came back, because his heart's purpose was to disciple men. He realized that the ministry was beneficial, even if the manner in which the work was being done was not altogether efficient. The following week, we went to Carson Section, the additional housing unit for Condemned Row. We made an agreement that first day that we wouldn't leave until we had spoken with each condemned man.

Benny and I, along with Larry Browning, a seminary student at Golden Gate Baptist Theological Seminary, ministered to the men in Carson Section every week for a few months. After a while, we started figuring out that guys were accepting the Lord. There were men with multiple personalities, men who were condemned on what I thought was flimsy evidence, men who were truly sorry for what they'd done, and a few men who were downright evil. We met with each and talked to him about Christ. Some were very receptive to what we were telling them; others steadily avoided us.

The only problem is we didn't have anywhere to conduct a Bible study on Death Row. There wasn't any room. The administration wanted us to conduct our ministry in the exercise yard, but that's where guys were lifting weights, playing basketball, smoking, cursing, and carrying on. There were too many distractions. In protest, Father Denis McManus, an Irish-Catholic priest, and I decided we would no longer do services on the exercise yard. The inmates filed federal suit against the California Department of Corrections for a death-row chapel and won. The state agreed to set up a chapel in the East Block Living Unit of Death Row, complete with seating for twenty-four.

A Dark Life

During one of our early Bible studies in the condemned visiting room, Benny was talking to the inmates about God's grace. Suddenly, Robert started crying, and the other inmates looked away, apparently embarrassed for him. After Robert regained his composure, he looked at me and asked, "Do you think God could even forgive someone like me?"

I said, "Robert, He can forgive anyone who asks."

That was how my relationship with Robbie began. Until then, he didn't believe God would have anything to do with him. When I met him, Robbie was a miserable soul. When he was previously incarcerated for manslaughter, his wife left him for a prison guard and took his son with them. He'd had no contact with his son for several years and didn't know where he was.

Robbie knew what he'd done was wrong. He'd had a violent and unhappy childhood from the day he came into the world. He was born three months premature after his mother was brutally assaulted by his drunken father, who kicked her in the stomach, and caused her to go into labor. Robbie told me that both of his parents beat him frequently; he'd suffered a broken jaw at the age of two after his father punched him.

Robbie's mother was a Cherokee from Oklahoma who started drinking whiskey when she was only eight. Kenneth Harris, his father, was awarded a Silver Star and Purple Heart for his service in World War II, but never seemed to recover from the stress of combat. For fun, his father would load a gun and tell Robbie and his siblings they had thirty minutes to hide before he would shoot them like animals.

After Robbie's family moved from Fort Bragg, North Carolina, to the San Joaquin Valley in California, his father was arrested in December 1964 for sexually abusing his daughters. His father was sent to prison, and Robbie, his mother, and many of his ten siblings were left to fend for themselves as migrant workers in the agricultural fields. By the time Robbie was a teenager, he'd had several run-ins with the police for offenses such as sniffing glue, killing animals, and stealing cars.

When Robbie was fourteen, his mother met another man, and threw Robbie out onto the streets. Robbie moved to Oklahoma to live with his older brother and sister. He was kicked out of school after attending classes for one day. After Robbie stole a car and fled to Florida, police picked him up and he spent the next four years as a ward in federal reformatories. He attempted suicide more than once and was diagnosed with schizophrenia.

Robbie was released from the reformatory when he turned nineteen, and moved to Chula Vista, California, where his father was. Robbie found a job as a welder, married his wife, and fathered a son. It seemed that he was turning his life around.

Within a year, however, Robbie was drinking heavily and unemployed. One night, Robbie and his oldest brother, Kenneth, fought with one of their neighbors in a trailer park. Robbie sprayed lighter fluid on the man and flicked matches at him. The man caught fire and died. Robbie pleaded guilty to manslaughter and served two-and-a-half years in the state prison at San Luis Obispo. He was released on parole, even though the sheriff where he lived testified he was in need of psychiatric attention.[4] Fewer than six months after Robbie was paroled in 1978, he and his brother kidnapped the teenage boys and killed them.

No Manual—Till Now

As San Quentin prepared for Robbie's execution in April 1990, I discovered there was no manual I could consult for counseling and ministering to the condemned, his or her family, or the victims' loved ones. There was a thirty-four-page manual, *Procedure 769*, which laid out in precise detail how to carry out an execution, but there was no plan that explained how to comfort those who are so greatly affected by it. So, I took it upon myself to write a Death Row ministry manual.

The manual described the proper procedures for ministering to condemned prisoners, including how to approach them, what not to ask (case facts), and that one shouldn't make promises. We needed to be consistent in terms of our availability; if the ministry was scheduled for Wednesday, we needed to be there on Wednesday. I talked about the Job principle, based on the righteous character in the Bible. When Job was cut down from family and success, his true friends came to him and just sat and listened. *Then* they spoke. A good chaplain has to learn to be an excellent listener.

I also wrote what I felt should be the protocol to follow as an execution approached. How should we minister to the staff? How should we work with the inmate, and how many chaplains should work with him? If the inmate chose an outside spiritual advisor, how could we, the institutional chaplains, help? I discussed how to minister to family members of both the victim and the inmate, as well as to the official witnesses.

I wrote the document and shared it with the warden. It was, for me, just a way to ensure that as a chaplain, I had all areas covered.

As I ministered to Robbie before his scheduled execution, he told me about his family and his son. Robbie told me that if he could have left San Quentin for one day, he would have gone to [his] father's grave and pissed on it.

As I visited with Robbie in the final days leading up to his death, I continued to talk to him about the Lord. He had accepted the Lord as his Savior in 1989, less than a year earlier. "What is it you really want to do?" I asked him. "What is important to you?"

He told me, "I just wish I could show these guys how much I love the Lord because I really do."

I asked Robbie if he had ever asked the families of his victims for forgiveness. Through his attorney, he sent letters to them. In the letters, Robbie wrote, "I deserve what I'm getting. I just want to ask you if you'll forgive me." Sharron Mankins, the mother of Michael Baker, responded and said she could forgive him, but she told him he deserved to die. Robbie thought she was fair. Mayeski's sister never responded to his letter.

Last Chances

On April 3, 1990, only hours before Robbie was scheduled to be strapped into a chair in the gas chamber, his lawyers obtained a stay of execution. The U.S. Supreme Court refused to lift a federal judge's order blocking his death. When Robbie received the news, he said, "Oh, thanks." He hugged two of his sisters and two other family members who came to San Quentin to be with him. The next day, prison guards accused him of having contraband—possibly drugs—and put him in solitary confinement for months.

Nearly two years later, the U.S. Supreme Court rejected Robbie's last appeal and his execution was scheduled for April 21, 1992. He knew there was nothing else his attorneys could do for him.

At the time I was ministering to Robbie, my family and I were living in a house on the San Quentin Prison grounds. My oldest daughter, Ebony, was eleven, and my oldest son, Earl Jr., was nine. Tamara was seven, and Franklin was four. The younger kids weren't old enough to understand what was happening, but I could sense that my two older children were worried. Robbie's fate weighed so heavily on my mind. As I talked to my children about the situation, I learned that Ebony was opposed to the death penalty, while Earl Jr. said he was in favor of it. I told Robbie about my kids' conflicting beliefs.

One night, as we ate dinner together as a family, the prison telephone rang. I answered it.

"It's Robert," Harris said. "How are you?"

"I'm fine. I'm eating dinner," I told him. "I'll be in to see you after I finish."

"I have a favor to ask you," he said. "I want to talk to your kids."

After considering his request for a moment and asking Angel if it was all right, I realized Robbie wouldn't say anything to hurt my children. I put Ebony on the phone first.

"You're right for being against the death penalty," Robbie told her. "Whatever you do for the rest of your life, stand up for your principles and don't let people change your mind."

Ebony handed the phone to Earl Jr.

"You're right for being for the death penalty," Robbie told him. "Whatever you do for the rest of your life, stand up for your principles and don't let people change your mind."

"Yes, sir," Earl Jr. said.

"Your dad brags about you being a great baseball player," Robbie said. "Go out and hit me a home run."

Two days later, I coached Earl Jr. in one of his Little League baseball games. He had a double and triple in his first two at-bats, then hammered the ball over the outfielders' heads in his third trip to the plate. We were already beating the other team badly, and I didn't want to run up the score. I stopped him at third base even though the ball hadn't yet been thrown into the infield. Earl Jr. started crying, and I'm sure everyone who noticed thought he was being selfish because I didn't let him score, but he was crying for another reason. "I promised Mr. Harris I'd hit him a home run," Earl Jr. told me. "I promised." When I told Robbie what happened, he told me to tell Earl Jr. that he "felt like it was a home run."

Incidentally, what Robbie said to my children may sound contradictory, but it wasn't. He told them to live their beliefs. I knew he thought, from our conversations, that they were feeling pressure and concern at school. He encouraged them to exhibit stand-up character. Angel and I were grateful for that.

Black Friday

On the morning of April 21, 1992, San Quentin Prison officials prepared to execute a condemned inmate for the first time in twenty-five years. In the past, executions at San Quentin always occurred on what became known as "Black Fridays." On the day an inmate is executed at San Quentin, the rest of the prison is locked down as the media, witnesses, and protestors converge on the correctional facility. The wardens always seemed to take a long weekend after executions.

Robbie's execution was scheduled for 12:01 A.M. For his last meal, he requested a bucket of Kentucky Fried Chicken, two pizzas with anchovies, Pepsi, and ice cream. His last meal was served at 6 P.M. Robbie also requested that each of the other thirty-three prisoners on his tier of Death Row receive a pint of ice cream. After Robbie finished his meal, he asked me to do one more thing for him.

"Can you find Mayeski's sister and ask her if she'll forgive me?" Robbie said. "She never responded to my letter."

I found Marilyn Clark, his sister, waiting for the execution with forty-seven other witnesses. She was the only member of her family who was there.

"Robert Harris asked me to ask you if you'll forgive him," I told her.

"Tell him I said no."

I went back to the cell where Robert was being kept. "What did she say?"

"Robert, she said no." I immediately saw a defeated look on his face. I tried to cheer him up by playing chess with him for the last time. Robert was in his cell, which included a mattress, chair, and toilet. I was outside his cell, playing chess through the bars. I knew I wouldn't allow him to beat me just because it was the last time we'd play. Our games of chess and dominoes had become pretty competitive over the years. That day was the last time I ever played a game of chess. I later realized that if I couldn't let a condemned man defeat me in his final game, chess had too much control over me.

Robbie and I were into our second game of chess when our time was cut short—the execution team arrived to take him to the gas chamber.

But, shortly before midnight, Robbie's execution was postponed for nearly four hours while federal courts considered appeals that execution by lethal gas was cruel and unusual punishment. Ultimately, a federal judge ordered Robbie's execution to be filmed to determine the extent of his suffering. His attorney called to tell him the news.

"I have some good news and bad news," the attorney told him. "The good news is you've got a stay of execution. The bad news is it's only for four hours."

Final Decision

Robbie's execution was rescheduled for 4:01 A.M. At about 3:00 A.M. guards brought him a new pair of blue jeans and a blue prison shirt to wear. At 3:30 A.M., a guard called the phone company to get the correct time and started the countdown. Before leaving his holding cell to walk fifteen paces to the gas chamber, Robbie told the four guards who would escort him to his death, "Guys, I know this is nothing personal. You're just doing your jobs. When I get to heaven, I'll put in a good word for you."

While Robbie's words may sound arrogant, he was actually ministering to the people around him, trying to give them words of encouragement. None of the people involved in Robbie's execution had ever participated in one before.

Warden Vasquez, who had arrived at San Quentin in 1984 and been there for much of Robbie's stay, was standing in the hall outside his cell. Robbie could tell that even the warden was nervous and said, "I had my doubts about you in the beginning, but Smitty says you're a good guy. He says you like to fish. I hope to fish with you in heaven one day."

Then Robbie looked at me and saw that I was in tears. "Smitty, if everything you've been telling me is true, there's going to be a white hearse waiting for me on the other side of that door," he said. The white hearse represented to Robbie the washing away of sin and forgiveness based on the verse that says, "Though your sins be as scarlet, God will make them white as snow."

At that moment, I realized Robbie was a changed man. He was trying to minister to us—in an attempt to ease our pain about what we were doing. As Robbie and I walked to the gas chamber, we simultaneously recited Psalm 23:

> The Lord is my shepherd; I shall not want. He maketh me to lie down in green pastures: he leadeth me beside the still waters. He restoreth my soul: he leadeth me in the paths of righteousness for his name's sake. Yea, though I walk through the valley of the shadow of death, I will fear no evil: for thou art with me; thy rod and thy staff they comfort me. Thou preparest a table before me in the presence of mine enemies: thou anointest my head with oil; my cup runneth over. Surely goodness and mercy shall follow me all the days of my life: and I will dwell in the house of the Lord forever.

Robbie had said that he'd accepted the Lord, and I wanted him to have the Word in him and he did.

At 3:48 A.M., the gas chamber's door opened. The four execution team members appeared and walked Robbie to a chair. There are actually two identical metal chairs with perforated seats, marked "A" and "B," inside the gas chamber. On a few occasions the state of California has executed two men at once. Robbie didn't put up a fight as he was lowered into the chair, then his arms, chest, and legs were strapped down by black restraints in a matter of seconds. Robbie's back was to the witnesses, so he strained to look for his older brother Randy, his close friend Michael Kroll, and three other friends. He nodded and gave them a thumbs-up. Robbie sat in the chair for twelve minutes, waiting to die, before another telephone call came. A U.S. appellate judge had issued another stay. Robbie was unstrapped from his chair and returned to his cell. It seemed so cruel to me.

After the last delay, the U.S. Supreme Court justices took the unprecedented action of ordering that no further stay would be valid unless it came from that court. At 6 A.M., prison spokesman Vernell Crittendon said through a peephole: "Warden, we are all in place." A couple of minutes later, with the sun rising above San Francisco Bay, Robbie was escorted back into the gas chamber.

The Moment

He was strapped into a chair again and a stethoscope was taped to his chest. The gas chamber's submarine-like door was closed and sealed at 6:05 A.M. Witnesses said Robbie seemed to mouth, "It's all right," and "I'm sorry."

Two minutes later, a prison official dropped a lever, lowering pellets of cheesecloth-wrapped sodium cyanide into two small buckets of sulfuric acid beneath the chair. Within seconds, Robbie began to inhale a fatal dose of lethal hydrocyanic gas as it rose from the holes in the chair. Dan Morain of the *Los Angeles Times*, who witnessed Robbie's execution, described the scene in the newspaper the next day:

> He just sat there, looking forward, hangdog. The first sign of death's beginning was a twitch of his hands, as if the rising gas had stung his skin. He inhaled and exhaled, four or five times. His head snapped back. His eyes rolled into his head. After 30 seconds, his head dropped, but he strained against the straps. Then his head rose as if by convulsion, then fell forward, slowly. After a minute, his hands appeared relaxed. A vein that runs the length of his forehead bulged, then looked as if it would burst. His mouth was wide open; his face flushed, then turned almost purple. He seemed oblivious at this point, perhaps two minutes into the execution. But then, as his body seemed to have relaxed, his head rose slowly and eerily . . . At 6:11, there was a cough, a convulsion, a line of drool. His balding pate was visible, as was his tightly banded and short ponytail.[5]

At 6:21 A.M., Vazquez declared Inmate B-66883 dead and announced to the witnesses the words by which Robbie had chosen to be remembered. I knew what the words were, because I'd written them on a piece of paper when the warden couldn't understand what Robbie was saying. The words were taken from the film *Bill and Ted's Excellent Adventure*: "You can be a king or a street sweeper, but everybody dances with the grim reaper."

Prison officials cleared the witnesses from the room, and I remained in the execution area after they left. The video camera was left on and the red light kept blinking as Robbie sat slumped in his chair. I exited the chamber area and as soon as I walked out, I saw a white Ram minivan. It was the hearse being used to transport Robbie's body. I remembered his words about the white hearse and a sense of momentary peace came over me. For me, the hearse was a reassurance of God's total involvement in the process. I did not want to be there, nor did I want to witness what I saw, yet the hearse made me understand deep inside that things would be all right. I knew that Robbie was okay.

I went next door to the visiting room, where the official witnesses were. As soon as I entered the room, a lady grabbed my neck. It was Marilyn Clark, Mayeski's sister. With tears in her eyes, she asked, "Did you tell him I forgave him?" I pulled away and looked into her eyes. "You told me to tell him no." It was a moment that will never leave me. After hearing her words, I realized she didn't get any closure from Robbie's death. She didn't let her anger go before he died, the way the Baker family did.

One might say that a murderer like Robert Harris did not deserve peace as he waited for his execution. However, as a Christian, I believe that every soul is worth saving and everyone can seek forgiveness if he opens his heart, becomes as a child, and asks. That's what Robert did in his final days. There was nothing manipulative about his desire to take ownership of his deeds; no matter what he wrote or said, he wasn't going to get off Death Row or get out of prison. He wanted to convey his remorse because he wanted to achieve some measure of God's pardon in the last days of his life.

As a man of God, I believe there's a redemptive value in everyone's life. I believe the death penalty and the entire process of capital punishment takes away the value of hope.

Cleared

Since 1973, 144 Death Row inmates have been released from prison because they were either acquitted or exonerated, according to the Death Penalty Information Center.[6] In California alone, six men sentenced to death under current California law were later cleared of the murder charges that put them on Death Row. I had four on my caseload who were actually innocent and went home:

- Jerry Bigelow spent eight years on Death Row after he was convicted of killing a man who'd picked him up while hitchhiking in 1980. Police pressured Jerry into confessing to the crime with the promise that he'd get a lenient sentence, and then he acted as his own attorney. He was twenty years old and had a ninth-grade education. After Jerry was convicted and spent eight years at San Quentin, he was acquitted of all charges in 1988, with the legal help of another inmate on Death Row. In his second trial, a defense attorney proved that a man who was hitchhiking with Jerry killed the driver while he was sleeping.

- Troy Lee Jones was convicted of killing a woman in Los Banos, California, on December 23, 1981. Police believed Jones had earlier killed an elderly neighbor, then murdered his girlfriend because he was afraid she would turn him in. The girlfriend's eight-year-old daughter testified that her mother told her that Troy killed the elderly woman, and a neighbor testified that she saw Troy and his girlfriend arguing about the killing. On appeal, the California Supreme Court overturned Troy's conviction because his legal defense was incompetent, and the prosecution dropped all charges in 1996. He was freed after spending fourteen years on Death Row.

- Lee Perry Farmer was convicted of fatally shooting an eighteen-year-old man in Riverside, California, in June 1981. He spent eighteen years on Death Row before the California Supreme Court overturned his conviction because his defense attorney had ignored the confession of Lee's co-defendant. On January 15, 1999, a jury acquitted Lee of murder in a retrial.

- Oscar Morris was accused of shooting a man at a bathhouse in Long Beach, California, on September 3, 1978. One of Oscar's acquaintances told police that Oscar committed the murder, and he was convicted of first-degree murder and sentenced to death in March 1983. Oscar's friend testified against him during the trial, but it was later revealed that the man had received a reduced sentence on auto theft charges in exchange for his testimony. In 1988, the California Supreme

Court reduced Oscar's sentence to life without parole, then the witness recanted his story from his deathbed in 1997. Oscar was released from San Quentin in 2000 after spending sixteen years on Death Row.

If a guy is on Death Row, and later released, what does that say about the system? It says that there's a flaw in it. If a guy can get there who shouldn't be there, the system isn't working.

No Relief

I think what most people don't understand is that capital punishment doesn't bring any more relief to a victim's family member than a life sentence does. Nearly every Death Row inmate would tell you he or she prefers the death penalty to a life sentence. They don't want to spend the rest of their lives behind bars. I don't believe capital punishment helps the victims' families and friends. Whenever someone is sentenced to death, there's an automatic appeal and the case is tried over and over again during the course of several years. Why would victims' families and friends want to keep reliving the pain of someone they loved being killed? Don't they want to move on?

If a murderer is sentenced to life in prison without the possibility of parole, the victims' families and friends will never hear from the killer again. Sure, capital punishment ensures that the condemned person dies. Yet the death of the victim remains unchanged. In many ways, a sentence of life without parole, when placed against the backdrop of the legal wrangling that comes with a death sentence, should be an option that is explained more often to victims' families. In my opinion, so-called closure should not be a part of the death penalty dialogue. It has nothing to do with peace of mind.

8

Death Row

A FEW WEEKS AFTER ROBBIE WAS executed, I went to see my aunt, Beatrice Clark, who was a minister. Shortly after I had been shot six times as a young man, Aunt Bee had come to my parents' home from Richmond, California, to see me. She anointed me with oil and prayed over me. She was a prayed-up, Holy Ghost–filled woman, and I loved her dearly.

"Baby, how you doing since that execution stuff?" she asked.

"I'm getting by," I told her.

"Well, baby, you know you're going to have to be with us when Michael Hill's time comes," she said.

I looked at her and asked, "Why would you want to be at an execution and why Michael Hill's?"

"You know, don't you?" she said. "That's who killed your cousins."

I told Aunt Bee, "You don't want to be there and you don't want to see that." She changed the subject.

On August 15, 1985, Hill robbed a jewelry store in Oakland, California, and killed two of my distant cousins, Anthony Brice Sr. and his four-year-old son, Anthony Brice Jr. Police said each was shot in the head at close range by a .38-caliber handgun. After police learned of Hill's potential involvement, they had him transported from a county jail, where he was serving time for a probation violation. He hadn't been in jail on the day my cousins were killed.

Initially, Hill told police that a drug dealer robbed the jewelry store. However, after police found the stolen jewelry and guns in the dealer's car and motel room, he told authorities that Hill had given him gold chains, watches, and cash to pay a six-hundred-dollar debt for cocaine. The dealer also told police he let Hill borrow a .38-caliber handgun to commit the robbery. Hill was convicted of two counts of murder with special circumstances and sentenced to death.

Hill was on my caseload at San Quentin Prison, but I had no idea he'd murdered my relatives. I had to inform my supervisor. I wrote letters to the prison warden and legal affairs coordinator, which were placed in a confidential file. Hill was removed from my caseload, and another chaplain took over the duties of ministering to him. Hill is still on Death Row.

After I started working at San Quentin, I rarely followed a high-profile murder case in the news if I believed there would be the possibility of capital punishment. I wanted to have an open mind when I encountered inmates sentenced to death. Being human, I realized that if I read about a heinous crime, I wouldn't want anything to do with the condemned prisoner. I also knew that by avoiding the men I would not be fulfilling my mission to take the gospel to the least of them.

The Condemned

There were thirteen men executed at San Quentin during my twenty-three years working as prison chaplain, but more than six hundred men were waiting for their execution dates, as their attorneys filed legal maneuvers in the Byzantine appeals process to try to save their clients' lives. An inmate's average length of stay on death row is about 17½ years. In 2006, shortly before I retired as chaplain at San Quentin, condemned inmate Michael Angelo Morales, who is on Death Row for a murder committed in the Stockton, California area, had his execution delayed because of his attorneys' claims that lethal injection was cruel and unusual punishment. Due to legal challenges to the state's lethal injection procedure, no inmate has been executed at San Quentin since 2006.

In July 2014, there were 728 men on San Quentin's Death Row and twenty women on Death Row (women are housed at the Central California Women's Facility in Chowchilla), the most by far of any state in the country. During my time behind the walls, I ministered to serial killers, murderers, rapists, and child predators. I prayed to God for mercy with dozens of men who had been sentenced to death. While many of their stories were shocking, frightening, and sickening, I believed it was my utmost duty to bring God's grace into their lives, one day at a time.

Here are the stories of the men who were executed during my time at San Quentin:

- David Edwin Mason was the first inmate executed at San Quentin after Robbie died. He was convicted of strangling and murdering four elderly people during separate robberies in 1980 and killing a fellow inmate in 1982. David asked to be executed and wanted to die. He knew he was guilty of the crimes and thought that execution was the best thing for him.

  In many ways, David had been trying to die his entire life. He tried to kill himself many times as a child, even setting his clothes on fire and throwing himself down stairs. He grew up in a strict Pentecostal home and was an unwanted child. His mother told the court that she tried to induce a miscarriage during her pregnancy with him by lifting furniture and riding horses. Both his parents abused him mentally and physically; David told me his father gave him fifty lashes with a belt every Friday in case he missed punishment during the week. After David's parents found him standing over his baby brother's crib with a knife, they locked him in a room they called the dungeon. His parents later shipped him away to foster homes and a juvenile hall, where David said other youths and administrators sexually molested him.

  At sixteen, David was convicted of setting a house on fire. A year later, he was kicked out of the United States Marine Corps. In 1977, David was arrested for robbing a convenience store and stabbing a clerk in the back with an ice pick. He was sentenced to three years in prison, and was released after serving a little more than half his sentence.

Shortly after David's release from prison, he killed and robbed five elderly people and attempted other crimes before police arrested him in February 1981. His first victim was Joan Pickard, a seventy-one-year-old woman whom he had known since childhood. He attended the same church as her family. Five months later, David strangled eighty-three-year-old Arthur Jennings and stole coins and jewelry. In November 1980, he killed seventy-five-year-old widow Antoinette Brown and, three weeks later, strangled and killed another widow, seventy-two-year-old Dorothy Lang, by beating her with a crescent wrench. David also confessed to shooting and killing fifty-five-year-old Robert Groff, a dog kennel owner, with whom he shared a trailer home. He never stood trial for murdering Groff.

Before police arrested David at a Holiday Inn, he recorded a long, rambling statement in which he confessed to killing the four elderly people in Oakland. On the tape, David said, "I know I'm going to die, and I don't care. In a way, I'm looking forward to it." He sent the tape to his parents, who turned it over to police. While David was awaiting trial, he and another inmate strangled their cellmate, twenty-four-year-old Boyd Wayne Johnson, with a knotted towel, and hung him from a heavy shower rod to make it look like suicide. In 1984, David was convicted of five murders and was sentenced to death.

After spending nine years on Death Row, David received his wish to die in the gas chamber on August 24, 1993. He was totally unreceptive to anything I tried to share with him about the gospel. He never participated in chapel or Bible study. I think his unwillingness to participate was a direct result of what happened to him growing up. David once showed me a scar in the shape of a cross on his calf. David said it had been carved into him so that he would be saved. David told me, "I have had enough of your Jesus."

Rev. Denis McManus, an Irish-Catholic priest, served as David's spiritual advisor. David spent his last day visiting with his family members. He refused a last meal and wanted only ice water while he waited in the deathwatch cell. Two minutes before midnight, a federal judge called the prison to make sure David's attorney was present in case David changed his mind about making a last-minute appeal. At 12:05 A.M., guards escorted him into the gas chamber. Three minutes later, Warden Daniel Vasquez asked David if he wanted to stop the execution. He answered, "No, warden, I want to proceed. Thank you, warden." David was pronounced dead at 12:23 A.M.

After David was executed, I started to wonder how many guys on death row were raised in a religious home, and at what age they no longer felt a need to go to church. I asked the condemned inmates to complete a survey, and the results showed that those who responded left church at the age of fourteen, and approximately 63 percent had grown up in a home with a parent who was a minister, evangelist, deacon, Sunday school teacher, or church choir member.

- William George Bonin was the first California inmate executed by lethal injection, after a federal court ruled the gas chamber to be inhumane. Bonin, a former truck driver, was known as the Freeway Killer, after he kidnapped, robbed, raped, and murdered at least fourteen boys in and around Los Angeles in 1979–1980 and dumped their bodies by roadways. Bonin showed no remorse for what he'd done. He was a brutal serial killer, stabbing his first victim more than seventy times and forcing another boy to swallow acid before killing him. He never apologized to his victims' families or asked for their forgiveness.

  In fact, when serial killer John Wayne Gacy was executed in Illinois on May 10, 1994, for sexually assaulting and murdering at least thirty-three teenage boys in Chicago during the 1970s, Bonin jumped up and down on the death row walk-alone yard. He started screaming, "[Now] it's me! It's me!" Once Gacy was executed, that left Bonin as the person currently on Death Row who had killed the most people. As hard as it might be to imagine, Bonin actually took pride in the fact that he'd killed more people than any other condemned inmate in the United States on Death Row at that time. Bonin didn't care about what he'd done to the boys; he just wanted the spotlight to be on him. For me, it was a sad indictment against mankind that someone was so self-absorbed in sin that he couldn't bring himself to seek forgiveness.

Rev. McManus served as Bonin's spiritual advisor, and I spent a lot of time with his victims' families and friends. It was so difficult for many of them to attend his execution on February 23, 1996. A lot of Bonin's victims were street kids, hitchhikers, and child prostitutes, aged twelve to nineteen. The murders ripped apart many of the families. You want to talk about pain? I can't imagine what it took from them at the time to look strong in the face of their sons' and brothers' killer. It was so tragic.

As a part of the ministry execution protocol I created, I spoke with the victims' family members, official witnesses, and the staff. Some of the victims' family members came with ombudsmen—people who offered support and aid to the family before and after they viewed the execution—from their counties, and some were by themselves.

When I went to the area where the group was waiting, I saw one young man who was clearly in emotional pain. I pulled him to the side, and asked if he wanted to go for a walk. We walked around the prison, including the area where we could see the protestors as well as the people supporting the execution. His brother was one of the victims. He talked about how the crime had damaged his mother and his family. He was a recovering addict. He said he really did not want to be there, but came as family support. As we continued to walk, I pointed out my house to him, and we could see my kids in the window looking out at the crowd. I realized the reason I was not in the back with Bill Bonin was because I was supposed to be with this young man. I stood with him as he watched Bill die. He cried and I cried.

For his final meal, Bonin requested two large pepperoni and sausage pizzas, three pints of coffee ice cream, and three six-packs of Coca-Cola. He watched *Jeopardy* as he waited to die. At 11:30 P.M., he gave his final words to the warden:

> I feel the death penalty is not an answer to the problems at hand. . . . I feel it sends the wrong message to the youth of the country. Young people act as they see other people acting instead of as people tell them to act. And I would suggest that when a person has a thought of doing anything serious against the law, that before they did, that they should go to a quiet place and think about it seriously.

Even in the end, Bonin didn't offer an apology for what he'd done. The first execution by lethal injection took four minutes, and Bonin was pronounced dead at 12:13 A.M.

- Keith Daniel Williams, a triple murderer, was executed about two months after Bonin was put to death. Williams, who was born prematurely to an alcoholic mother, and was diagnosed with fetal alcohol syndrome, was convicted of killing two men and a pregnant woman in Merced, California, on November 20, 1978. He had agreed to purchase a car from one of the men at a rummage sale only to return to the victims' house two days later and demand the return of his check. Williams killed the two men execution-style, then kidnapped the woman and raped and shot her multiple times on a secluded hillside.

  Peggy Harrell, director of Marin County's Prisoner Services, was Williams's spiritual advisor. Lourdes Meza, the woman he killed, had four children; they attended the execution. I spent a lot of time with them before Williams was executed. After Williams was declared dead at 12:08 A.M. on May 3, 1996, one of her daughters turned to me and asked, "Is that it? It looked like he just went to sleep."

- Thomas Martin Thompson was executed on July 13, 1988, for allegedly raping and killing a woman in 1981. To this day, I still believe that Tommy was innocent. Most guys on death row don't say they're innocent; they confess to their crimes and show remorse. At the time he was executed, Tommy was the only condemned inmate during my tenure to maintain his innocence until the end.

Father McManus and I spent hours discussing Tommy. He was forthright, polite, and showed something that we thought was a bit unusual for death row: concern for others. From time to time, he would tell us about a guy who screamed throughout the night, or someone he could hear talking to himself for hours on end.

Thompson, who had no prior criminal or violent history, was convicted of killing twenty-year-old Ginger Fleischli in Laguna Beach, California, on September 11, 1981. Thompson shared an apartment with the woman, and police say he murdered her after raping her. Thompson told police he had consensual sex with the woman after they'd spent an evening at a pizza parlor drinking beer, whiskey, and rum and smoking hashish. Tommy told police he passed out and the woman was gone when he woke up the next morning. He was arrested by police in Mexico and returned to the United States.

Another man, David Leitch, who was with Thompson and Fleischli on the night she was killed, was also convicted of her murder and was sentenced to fifteen years to life in prison. Leitch had known Fleischli for years and had a previous romantic relationship with her. Police found Leitch's shoe print near her body, and discovered matching carpet fibers from her apartment in the trunk of his car.

Nonetheless, a jury convicted Tommy of murder after only eight hours of deliberations. A judge sentenced Tom to death because he was also convicted of the rape charge, which made it a special circumstances crime. In 1995, a U.S. district judge overturned the rape conviction and wrote in his decision that the circumstances of Thompson's conviction left him with an "unsettling feeling" about executing him. But a federal appeals court reinstated the rape conviction, and then the U.S. Supreme Court voted 5–4 to uphold the appellate court's ruling.

After a seventeen-year fight to stay alive, Thompson was out of appeals and became resigned to his fate. His last meal included Alaskan king crab with melted butter, spinach salad, pork fried rice, Mandarin-style pork spare ribs, a hot fudge sundae, and a six-pack of Coca-Cola. Tommy died at 12:06 A.M., about five minutes after a lethal trio was injected into his veins: sodium pentothal to put him to sleep, pancuronium bromide to stop his breathing, and potassium chloride to stop his heart. His last words were: "For seventeen years, the attorney general has been pursuing the wrong man. In time, he will come to know this. I do not want anyone to avenge my death. Instead, I want you to stop killing people. God bless." His sister planned to spread his ashes near the Little Mermaid statue that greets returning sailors in Copenhagen, Denmark, his ancestral homeland.

• I didn't think they would execute Jaturun Siripongs because he was a foreigner. Siripongs was raised in a brothel in Thailand after his parents separated. His first brush with the law occurred when, as a twenty-year-old, he was shot in the head while robbing a department store in Thailand. He recovered and served time in a Thai prison. Later, he trained as a monk in a Buddhist monastery. "Jay" took a job as a cook on a cargo ship and earned passage to America by helping the U.S. government in a sting operation.

Police accused Siripongs of robbing a market where he worked in Garden Grove, California, on December 15, 1981. He was accused of strangling shop owner Packovan "Pat" Watanaporn and stabbing clerk Quach Nguyen, killing them both. When police arrested him, they found the market owner's credit cards and jewelry at his apartment. Siripongs admitted to robbing the store but claimed an accomplice killed them. He never revealed the identity of the alleged accomplice.

Jay seemed to be a very peaceful and amicable man. He was a model prisoner and never showed a sign of violence. Siripongs meditated and prayed daily, and became an accomplished painter during his nearly sixteen years on Death Row. Before Jay was executed on February 9, 1999, myriad people appealed for clemency, including Pope John Paul II and Thailand's ambassador to the United States. Even two of the jurors who convicted him and the widower of one of his victims appealed for mercy on his behalf.

But California Governor Gray Davis, who was barely a month into office, denied Jay's bid to commute his sentence to life in prison. During his campaign, Davis promised to be tough on criminals and vowed he was pro-death penalty. After the U.S. Supreme Court rejected two appeals for a stay of execution, Jay died of lethal injection at 12:19 A.M. He spent his final moments with Ajahn Pasanno, a co-abbot from the Abhayagiri Buddhist Monastery in Redwood Valley, California.

• As surprised as I was about Siripongs's execution, I was saddened by the fate of Manuel Babbitt. Manny was a Vietnam veteran who lived through the seventy-seven-day siege of Khe Sanh, one of the war's bloodiest battles. He served two tours in Vietnam and was a changed man, for the worse, when he returned home.

Manny had a fragile mind before he was thrown into combat. He was raised in dirt-poor Wareham, Massachusetts, among a small community of immigrants from the Cape Verde Islands. His father was an alcoholic who physically abused his mother and his children. When Manny's father died when he was fourteen, his mother suffered a breakdown. She was often seen talking to a pear tree in the yard, and wore mourning for several years.

During the Vietnam War, Manny rose to the rank of corporal in the U.S. Marines and was part of an armored car unit. He was wounded by shrapnel at Khe Sanh and flown to a medical unit by helicopter atop a pile of bodies. After Manny was married and served a second tour of duty, something went terribly wrong. While Manny was stationed at a base in Rhode Island, he killed rabbits with his M-16 rifle, and skinned them, while conducting night patrols. On some nights, he would scream at his wife to take their babies and run for cover from bombs. He was suffering from what we now know to be post-traumatic stress disorder.

After Manny was dishonorably discharged from the Marines, he turned to a life of crime. He was convicted of committing twenty-eight burglaries and two armed robberies. He spent time at the infamous Bridgewater State Hospital for the Criminally Insane, in Massachusetts, where he was diagnosed as a paranoid schizophrenic.

After moving to California to be closer to his brother, Manny broke into an apartment in Sacramento and beat and sexually assaulted seventy-eight-year-old Leah Schendel on December 18, 1980. She suffered significant injuries and died of a heart attack. Police say he tried to rape another woman the next night. Manny's brother turned him in to police after he found a cigarette lighter bearing the initials "L. S." among his possessions.

Manny was sentenced to death on July 6, 1982. He spent nearly seventeen years on Death Row before he was executed on May 4, 1999. More than six hundred fellow Marines signed a petition to have his sentence commuted to life in prison. Manny was awarded a Purple Heart for his wounds in Vietnam while he was imprisoned on death row. He waived his last meal, choosing to fast for forty-eight hours, and asked prison officials to donate the fifty-dollar stipend to homeless Vietnam veterans. Manny didn't want anyone with him when he was executed. He didn't want anyone in the holding cell or in the execution chamber. He died alone. Manny's last words were: "I forgive all of you."

I will always see Manny's face. When my children were small, we had a family portrait taken. I was talking with Stevie Lamar Fields, who was also on my death row caseload, and showed him the picture. Stevie said, "You should get Buck to paint a picture for you." I took the picture to Buck Reilly and asked him if he could paint it. He said he would try but admitted that he'd never painted a portrait. As the picture was being painted, Buck had a problem: he could not distinguish my son Franklin's face. Franklin was a baby and the picture I gave him was small. So, Buck got Manny to pose for the picture. Buck figured that since Manny had the same facial features and complexion, it might work. It did work and the picture sits in my living room today.

• I didn't have a lot of interaction with Darrell Keith Rich, who was known as the "Hilltop Rapist" after he had savagely raped and killed four women and girls and sexually assaulted five others during a two-month crime spree in Cottonwood, California, in 1978. While Rich was on death row, he learned that his biological father had an Indian heritage, so he claimed to be one-fourth Cherokee. Shortly before Rich was executed on March 15, 2000, his lawyers fought unsuccessfully to allow him to participate in a sweat lodge ceremony. There was actually a sweat lodge at San Quentin, but death row inmates weren't allowed to use it because of security risks.

Rich's victims included eleven-year-old Annette Selix. After Rich raped Selix, he threw her—still alive—off a 105-foot high bridge. He also beat one of his victims to death with a rock and shot a mother twice in the mouth as she pleaded for her life. His last word was "Peace."

- Robert Lee Massie was the only man ever to serve two sentences on death row at San Quentin. His first death sentence came after he committed a series of robberies and assaults in Los Angeles during a nine-day crime spree in January 1965. First, he robbed a man on the front lawn of his home and shot him, grazing the side of his head. Later that night, Massie shot and killed a woman while he was robbing her and her husband as they climbed out of their car at their home. He also robbed a bar and shot another man in a hotel room. Massie was arrested and was convicted of murder, attempted murder, and robbery. A judge sentenced him to death.

  Massie was scheduled to die in 1967 and was so close to his execution that he'd ordered his last meal and written a will. But then-California Governor Ronald Reagan granted a stay of execution so that Massie could testify for his getaway driver. Massie fought the stay but was transported to Los Angeles, where he told jurors the man wasn't with him on the night he killed the woman. After Massie returned to San Quentin, the California Supreme Court temporarily suspended executions, then the U.S. Supreme Court declared them unconstitutional in 1972. Massie and more than one hundred other condemned inmates had their death sentences commuted to life in prison with the possibility of parole.

While the legal battle was raging around him, Massie repeatedly said that he was ready to die and didn't want to spend the rest of his life in prison, yet he wrote an article for *Esquire* magazine in which he called capital punishment anti-Christian and politically motivated. It was always very difficult to understand his thinking. During the time he was on my caseload, I realized that he played a lot of mind games.

Then, in a bizarre turn of events, Massie was awarded parole in 1978. A few months later, he killed a man and shot another while robbing a liquor store in San Francisco on January 3, 1979. He was convicted of murder and attempted murder and was sentenced to death a second time.

Massie prided himself on being somewhat of a jailhouse lawyer. There was a young man on the row, Jerry Bigelow, to whom Massie took a liking. Bigelow was sentenced to death in 1980 and, with Massie's help, his murder conviction and death sentence were overturned. Jerry, on death row for eight years, was acquitted of murder at his retrial in 1988.

On March 27, 2001, Massie was executed by lethal injection—more than three decades after he was originally sentenced to die. It was the end of an unforgettable life. Massie had been born to teenage parents in Virginia. According to his attorneys, his mother was fifteen and his father married her only to avoid being charged with statutory rape. His parents fed him liquor and drugs until he was five. Massie was removed from their home and spent time in eleven foster homes, including one in which his foster parents disciplined him by holding his head under water in a toilet. He was already a criminal by the time he moved to California.

Massie prided himself on being a racist and country boy, and thought his prejudice would turn me off from trying to share the gospel with him. But I discovered that he had been a chaplain's clerk at San Quentin. I gave books to inmates, and eventually Massie asked me for some.

What I learned about Massie was that doing time did not bother him. There's a distinct difference between regeneration and rehabilitation. Massie never owned up to his responsibility for the first murder, but the system declared that he was rehabilitated. Even while working in the chaplain's office, he never expe-

rienced regeneration. Sadly, somebody else was murdered after he was released from prison.

- Like so many other condemned inmates at San Quentin, Stephen Wayne Anderson had a tragic childhood.
According to court records, he was physically abused.
His mother was a coal miner's daughter and his father
was an alcoholic oil worker. His mother often told her
two sons that she dreaded the days they were born,
and even told neighbors that she preferred her dogs to
her children. When Stephen was fourteen, his father
threw him out of the house. He lived in the hills surrounding Farmington, New Mexico, and never went
home again.

  Anderson was sentenced to prison in Utah in the
mid-1970s for multiple counts of aggravated burglary.
While he was incarcerated at Utah State Prison, he
killed an inmate, assaulted another inmate, and beat a
correctional officer. He escaped from prison on November 24, 1979, and was on the lam for more than
six months. On May 26, 1980, Stephen broke into a
home in San Bernardino, California. His attorneys
claimed that he didn't think anyone was home, that he
shot and killed an eighty-one-year-old retired piano
teacher only after she awoke and startled him. After
shooting the woman in the face, Anderson went to the
kitchen and cooked himself noodles and poured a glass
of milk. He was arrested at the home, and sentenced to
death on July 24, 1981.

While Stephen was at San Quentin, prison psychologists discovered he had an IQ of 136. He became an accomplished poet and wrote several novels while serving more than two decades on death row. He was a quiet man we called "Sonny." His attorneys argued that he was a changed man, and the daughters of the woman he killed and the mother of the Utah inmate he murdered even asked that his life be spared.

Stephen was part of my Bible study group on death row, along with Donald Beardslee, Manny, Robbie, and Tommy, but during the week before Sonny was executed on January 29, 2002, he became withdrawn and remained alone in his cell. He stopped seeing his spiritual advisors five days before he was executed and then turned away visitors altogether. After Sonny died, one of his attorneys released one of his poems, entitled, "Unchained Visions, #9." It read:

> *If no other misses you, I will:*
> *I will sense the emptiness*
> *Where once you breathed*

- Donald Beardslee was a three-time killer who stabbed, choked, and drowned a woman in her bathtub in his native St. Louis in December 1969. After serving about ten years for killing the woman in St. Louis, he shot and killed a twenty-three-year-old woman and slashed the throat of a nineteen-year-old woman after a botched drug deal in Redwood City, California, in

1981. The women were killed in revenge for a $185 drug debt owed to one of Beardslee's associates.

Beardslee's attorneys argued that he'd been brain damaged since birth, but California Governor Arnold Schwarzenegger and the federal courts didn't buy it. After serving more than twenty years on Death Row, Beardslee was executed on January 19, 2005. There were no last words.

Donald was close to Benny, who volunteered to help the chaplains on Death Row, and wrote him letters from time to time. Some years after Donald was executed, a letter arrived at Benny's house. Apparently, someone had found the letter in a ditch in Ceres, California, addressed to Ben Hardister at "Sonoma Plaza Realty, In Sonoma, California." Benny had closed that office ten years before the letter arrived. The person who found the letter took it to the post office and a high-school friend of Benny's who was working there saw the letter. Knowing that the office was closed, he dropped it off at Benny's house. In the letter, Donald talked about his love of Christ, the 49ers, and how important Benny's visits and words were to him. As Benny said, "Wow, words of encouragement from the grave."

- The execution of Stanley "Tookie" Williams on December 13, 2005, was one of the most politically charged in U.S. history. Tookie was one of the founding members of the Hoover Crips street gang in Los

Angeles, which had been formed by his high-school friend Raymond Washington. Tookie had moved to Los Angeles with his mother in 1959, after his father deserted his family in New Orleans before Tookie's first birthday.

On February 28, 1979, Tookie and three companions smoked cigarettes laced with PCP and robbed a 7-Eleven convenience store. As the robbery was taking place, police alleged, Tookie took the clerk, Albert Owens, into a back room and shot him in the back twice. Owens was an Army veteran and father of two children. Less than two weeks later, Williams broke down the door of a hotel and killed the owners, two Taiwanese immigrants, and their daughter. The two robberies netted $220.

Williams was convicted of four counts of murder and two counts of robbery by a Los Angeles Superior Court jury and sentenced to death in 1981. In 1987, after a string of violent incidents involving guards and fellow inmates at San Quentin, he was placed in solitary confinement for six and a half years. When Tookie finally emerged from the hole, he was a changed man. He'd spent much of his time in solitary confinement reading a dictionary, the Bible, and books about African-American history. He started to reflect on his own life and the mistakes that had put him on death row.

One day in 1989, my sister Sylvia called me about a young man housed in the California Youth Authority facility where she worked. His name was William

Hansbrough. "Little Will" was a Crip and proud of his street reputation. He was being detained for attempted murder. My sister heard him talking about his big homey, Tookie, and how Tookie was his main man. She asked if I would come to the facility and visit with William.

I went to see him on a Saturday, and when I got there he came into the room sagging and bragging. I just looked at him, a little boy, and asked, "How can Big Took be your main man? He's been in prison almost as long as you've been living." Little Will thought Tookie was like a god. He thought of him as this massive figure who killed other inmates. In his mind, Tookie was this fantastically dangerous character.

I left the facility with a mission: to get Little Will to see another side of Stanley "Tookie" Williams. The next week, I shared the story about Little Will with Tookie and the warden. Tookie wrote Little Will a letter telling him he was still young and when he got out, he should take advantage of his second chance at life. I gave the letter to my sister and she shared it with Little Will.

In March 2010, I was reading the *Los Angeles Times* and came across a story that brought tears to my eyes. William Hansbrough, a thirty-six-year-old black man, had been strangled March 4 in his county jail cell. At the time of his death, Hansbrough was incarcerated at the Twin Towers jail on charges of possessing a firearm as an ex-felon. Hansbrough had been sharing a cell with Jamar Tucker, a twenty-six-year-old black man, whom authorities described as his friend and fellow 107-Hoover gang member.

In his final years on Earth, Tookie really worked to curb gang violence. In 1993, he taped a message from prison that was broadcast to L.A. gang members at a peace summit. Tookie also coauthored eight children's books in which he urged kids to stay away from street gangs and violence. He wrote two memoirs and was working on two more books when he was executed. Tookie probably did more than anyone else to help stop street-gang violence. He was even nominated for a Nobel Peace Prize. Everyone from South African Bishop Desmond Tutu to rapper Snoop Lion urged Schwarzenegger to commute his death sentence to life in prison without the possibility of parole.

The governor declined to act, and Tookie was executed by lethal injection shortly before Christmas Day in 2005. Bishop Donald Green, the senior pastor at the San Francisco Christian Center, and Dr. Anthony Williams, senior pastor at Maranatha Christian Center in San Jose, California, ministered to Tookie during his time on death row. When it became clear that Tookie would be executed, Rev. Jesse Jackson spent some time with him before he died.

• Clarence Ray Allen was one of the oldest men ever executed. When the seventy-six-year-old Allen was killed by lethal injection on January 17, 2006, he couldn't walk and had to use a wheelchair. He was legally blind from diabetes and had suffered a heart attack only a few months earlier. Allen's attorneys argued that putting him to death wouldn't do society any good, and they may have been right.

Allen, who grew up in Oklahoma and worked cotton fields to make a living, eventually moved to Fresno, California, and became a very successful businessman. He owned and operated a security firm and became wealthy. He bought Arabian show horses and airplanes and had a sprawling ranch with a swimming pool. However, Allen was leading a double life. He used his access from the security firm to orchestrate robberies at businesses and residences he'd been hired to protect.

In June 1974, Allen and two of his employees robbed a grocery store in Fresno. He had lifted the alarm key from the pocket of the storeowners' son during a pool party. When his son's girlfriend told the storeowners what happened, Allen instructed an associate to kill her. Allen was arrested nearly three years later after a botched robbery of a Kmart store, and police connected him to the earlier burglary and killing. He was sentenced to life in prison in 1978.

While serving time at Folsom State Prison, Allen conspired with a fellow inmate, Billy Ray Hamilton, to murder the people who'd testified against him. Shortly after Hamilton was released from prison in 1980, he and his girlfriend killed three young people at the grocery store Allen had robbed in Fresno. When police picked up Hamilton a few days later, he was carrying a hit list of the people Allen wanted him to kill. Allen was charged with three counts of murder and conspiring to kill seven witnesses. He was sentenced to death in 1982. After he spent more than twenty-three years on Death Row, Allen's final words were: "Hoka hey, it's a good day to die."

Clarence, or "Chief," as we called him, had been an Assembly of God preacher and knew the Word of God. This occurred when he was younger and before he started committing crimes. Sometime during his detention on death row, though, he discovered that he was Native American and stopped participating in Bible study. In the midst of his rebellion from God, he started to commit crimes. He felt somehow that if he served God on the surface, things would work out for him. To me, Chief is an example of what can happen to any of us, if we fail to live out the calling God has placed on our lives.

While the men who were executed at San Quentin during my watch were convicted of many heinous crimes, I found some of them to be souls crying out in emotional pain. Some of the men on Death Row came to look at me as their mentor. Stevie Fields saw me as a brother he could talk to. Andre Burton said I taught him that it was okay to have faith. Billy Ray Hamilton saw me as a guy who did not allow his racism to keep me from offering him the same care I gave the other inmates. I hope they saw me as someone who might be able to help them turn their lives around during their last days on Earth.

In my mind, each of us, from the day we are born, is on death row. We don't know the time or the hour when we are going to die, but each of us must take a final breath and walk a last step. I continued to ask the men I ministered to the same question: "Where will you be when you get where you are going? Where will you spend eternity?" I think it's a question everyone needs to ask him- or herself.

9

The Baseball Experiment

AFTER MORE THAN A DECADE of working as the chaplain at San Quentin Prison, I was still searching for ways to connect with the inmates. Having spent so much time inside the walls, I'd reached the conclusion that prison is about punishment, not rehabilitation. Being sentenced to life in prison, or even death, means being held captive, and I wanted to find ways to offer inmates an outlet from the mundane rituals of incarceration. I don't think people understand how maddening life in prison can be. You wake up in the same bed, wear the same clothes, complete the same tasks, and eat the same meals every day. As others have said, the clock moves slowly in prison: it's as if the pages of the calendar never turn.

I was involved in the sports programs at San Quentin for several years. I coached the defensive line and linebackers on the prison's eight-man tackle football team. We played against military teams from the local bases. I played chess and dominoes with inmates. I came to understand that it was my job to preach only when I had inmates inside the chapel. When I was outside the chapel, I spent my time trying to get the inmates to come in. I learned that the best way to do it was to spend time with inmates while participating in activities they enjoyed.

Sports programs have been an important part of the rehabilitation process at San Quentin for many years. Inmates play basketball, tennis, soccer, and other sports at the prison yard. I believe sports offer them a way to stay in shape physically, as well as an opportunity to relieve the stress that comes with being isolated from their families and living in such a dangerous place.

Bringing Baseball Back

When I walked into the Catholic chapel one day, I noticed the clerk, Jimbo, had a catcher's glove sitting in the window of his office.

"What are you doing with a catcher's glove?" I asked.

"I play baseball," he told me.

"Do you play here?"

"No, there's not a field," he said.

Growing up as a big baseball fan, I understood the benefits of the game. It requires teamwork, as well as personal responsibility, because there are nine moving parts on the field. I also believed baseball might go a long way toward cooling the racial tension inside the prison.

San Quentin has always been racially segregated. The inmates were housed in separate cells based on race or gang affiliation, and remained in separate groups in the dining hall, prison yard, and seemingly everywhere else. Blacks rarely mixed with whites, whites rarely mixed with Hispanics, and the Hispanics rarely mixed with Asians or Pacific Islanders. Though San Quentin is a melting pot of different ethnic groups, there is little racial mingling. If a white guy is caught hanging out with a black guy, the Aryan Brotherhood might have him killed.

After my conversation with Jimbo, I asked Warden Daniel Vasquez about bringing baseball back to San Quentin. The sport had been played inside the prison since the late nineteenth century. In fact, former major league pitcher Charlie Sweeney played on the prison team after he was convicted of killing a man in a saloon brawl in the 1890s. In 1913, Warden James Johnston gave the team uniforms instead of prison stripes, and arranged for the squad to play in a recreation league. In the early 1940s, manager Connie Mack arranged to have the Philadelphia A's play an exhibition game against the San Quentin squad during spring training.

Believe it or not, there were several good baseball players at San Quentin over the years. In 1979, the San Francisco Giants invited Curtis Charles, a paroled ex-con from San Quentin, to spring training after he played on the prison team. Here's what Charles said about playing baseball in prison: "At the 'Q' we had rocks, glass, knives, and razor blades on the field. I'm not kidding! One day last year, I tried to smooth the dirt with my foot and kicked a knife someone had stashed."

This didn't discourage me. I knew the yard was going to have weapons no matter what. It was prison and guys hid things. Mike

Egan recently reminded me how many knives we found while prepping the field.

Once I explained the benefits of baseball to Vasquez, he told me that if I could get the inmates to agree to play together, he'd give me permission to construct a baseball diamond on the lower yard. When I first approached a group of inmates about organizing a baseball team, I heard the complaints I expected: the blacks didn't want to play with the whites; the whites didn't want to play with the blacks, and so on. I told them to go talk to their groups about the idea and get back to me. Much to my surprise, every group agreed to allow its members to play on the baseball team without repercussions.

If You Build It, They Will Play

It took nine months for us to build a baseball field. It was a difficult task, because the prison wouldn't let us use power equipment. We had to persuade the administration to give us shovels, rakes, picks, and hoes; they're normally considered "weapons stock" and inmates aren't allowed to have them. Jerry "Wolf" Stipe, who was part of the so-called white group, had a knack for finding whatever we needed. He didn't play on the team, but loved baseball and wanted to help. Eventually, we had a baseball field, after a couple of dozen inmates provided the labor to build the infield and pitching mound. It didn't cost California's taxpayers a dime.

We had open tryouts in the summer of 1994 and about thirty inmates showed up. It didn't take us long to figure out who could play and who couldn't. Once we settled on a roster of about twenty players, I told the team what we were going to call ourselves: the Pirates. "Pirates are swashbucklers," I told them. "Pirates come in and steal people's dreams!" I wanted to motivate the guys to see themselves as able to do the impossible, able to get a victory even when the odds were against them. I laid out the ground rules for being a member of the team: If a player received a disciplinary report, caused a disturbance in his cellblock, or missed work, he was off the team. I told the players they also would be responsible for maintaining and manicuring the field.

After a few months of practice, I thought we were finally ready to play a game. Getting an outside team to come into San Quentin to play a game wasn't easy. It probably didn't help that visiting players were informed by guards at the arrival gate that the administration wouldn't negotiate for their release in a hostage situation. One of the first teams that played us on a regular basis was aptly named "The Willing." San Quentin can be pretty intimidating, especially for someone who has never been there before.

On October 8, 1994, the San Quentin Pirates played their first game against a San Francisco Giants fantasy league team. The opposition consisted mostly of white-collar professionals, including lawyers, engineers, accountants, and other guys who could afford to pay the cost of the Giants' fantasy camp. Many of them had played college baseball. Duane Kuiper, a former Giants second baseman, and Mike Krukow, an-ex Giants pitcher, coached the fantasy team and ended up playing in the game. They were partners on the Giants' radio broadcast; sports-talk radio host Ralph Barbieri told them that we were having problems finding opponents, so they organized a team to play us.

Before the first pitch, I laid out San Quentin's unique ground rules for our visitors. I told them that if a fly ball flew over the fence in left field and landed in the recreation yard it was a home run. If a fly ball to right-center landed in the Native American reservation, it was a homer (we eventually had to put up a net to keep balls away from the Indian sweat lodge). And if a ball cleared the orange traffic cone in a straightaway center on the fly, it also was a home run. The umpire, an inmate, also advised Kuiper about his not-so-liberal strike zone: "It will be determined by whom I eat with every day and it's not you guys."

We played exceptionally well in our first game. Our pitcher, M. J. Moore from Oakland, threw a gem. Our shortstop, Leonard Neal from Richmond, California, relieved him late in the game and gave up a homer to Kuiper, which was only the second one he'd ever hit in a game (he'd hit only one in nearly 3,400 at-bats in twelve major league seasons). Warning sirens, which meant that there was an institution emergency, interrupted the game twice, and inmates had to drop to a knee and remain still until the siren stopped. After all the commotion, we held on for a 9–8 victory.

Many of the spectators in the recreation yard, including inmates of myriad races, cheered and jumped up and down after we won. Some guys were bummed out because they had bet against us. Slowly but surely, baseball brought the prisoners closer together. Even if someone wasn't playing, he was cheering for somebody who was representing him. At times, we had a black pitcher, a Mexican catcher, an Asian-American outfielder, and a white infielder. I knew if we could break down the barriers of race, religion, and gang affiliation, San Quentin would be a much better place.

We played one more game during the 1994 season, and played about fifteen games the next year. We played the Oakland Oaks, a thirty-five-years-and-older team, in the first game in 1995 and they became our opening-day opponent every season. Eventually, we played thirty to forty games per year—each of them at home (go figure).

In 2000, I changed the name of our team from the Pirates to the Giants, but not without controversy. I was working as chaplain for the San Francisco Giants, and equipment manager Mike Murphy and assistant general manager Ned Colletti were generous enough to donate their spring training uniforms. When I broke the news to our team, a couple of players weren't too happy. Our team captain, Jason Gottlieb, threw down his glove and walked back to his cell. Dan Jones, one of the coaches, went to talk to him. Jason said he was a Pirate "through and through," but Dan was able to talk him into coming back. Gottlieb, who kept a baseball encyclopedia of newspaper clippings in his cell, was a Los Angeles Dodgers fan and didn't want to be a Giant. Eventually, every one of the guys liked having a new uniform, though. We decided to field two teams after that: the Giants and the Pirates, which consisted of guys who hadn't played much baseball before.

Better Stadium, Stellar Team

In 2002, Mike Egan, Scott Burkman, and Mike Orren of Sport Choice, who built the baseball diamond at what is now AT&T Park in San Francisco, were kind enough to build us a new stadium at San Quentin. Using inmate labor, they dug more than six inches deep in the lower yard to find soft dirt. Along the way, they found at least three shanks that had been hidden in the soil. A prison guard walked with them step by step. Metallica, who played a benefit concert at San Quentin, donated ten thousand dollars to the baseball program. The Grateful Dead's Rex Foundation also provided the team's first set of uniforms, before we were given the Giants' hand-me-downs.

Slowly, our field was coming together. We still didn't have an outfield fence, but we rolled out a temporary fence, like the ones used on highways, every time we played a game. Bryan Smith, one of our co-captains, built a scoreboard. Anthony "Tone" Jackson, who grew up near me in Stockton, California, helped paint the scoreboard and erected it in right field. It read: "San Quentin's Field of Dreams."

I found an old friend, Mel Carriere, and he agreed to be our pitching coach. Mel was well known in Marin County for his compassion and knowledge of the art of pitching. He also was the person who helped move Project IMPACT (more on that in chapter 13) from an idea to a nonprofit. We needed a pitching coach to take our team to the next level, and Mel was the man for the job.

We opened the new stadium in 2003, and Chris Rich, one of our new pitchers, hit a home run in the first game. Chris, who stood about six feet eight inches tall, was part of our Murderers' Row—literally. He had been a star pitcher at St. John's University in New York. He helped the Johnnies reach the College World Series in Omaha, Nebraska in 1978 and 1980. In 1979, he had the lowest earned-run average among NCAA Division I pitchers and actually outperformed his teammates John Franco and Frank Viola, who would become Major League Baseball stars.

But, before Chris's senior season in 1981, he was pitching batting practice without a protective net in front of him. A line drive hit his left shin, breaking it, and the bone never fully healed. Chris tried to come back and pitch, but he ended up hurting his throwing arm while compensating for the pain in his leg. His dream of pitching in the majors was over.

After graduating from St. John's, Chris moved to California and worked as an electrician for his brother's security company. He married his wife, Sharon, but then battled depression and alcoholism. In the spring of 1995, after Chris argued with his wife about an unpaid bill, he crushed her skull with an aluminum baseball bat while she slept. He tried to cover up the crime, dressing her in hiking clothes and dropping her body in a drainage ditch near a canyon outside San Bernardino, California. Chris filed a missing persons report with the police and even helped lead search parties through the hills. After failing a lie-detector test, though, he finally admitted murdering his wife. Chris was sentenced to twenty-six years to life and isn't eligible for parole until 2016.

Chris spent the first several years of his sentence at Corcoran State Prison, but requested a transfer to San Quentin after he heard about our baseball team. He hadn't been able to throw a baseball for several years because of a torn rotator cuff, but once he got back into shape he was our best pitcher. I'm not sure what made Chris snap the night he killed his wife, but he was a model prisoner and teammate. He designed scorecards for our team and counseled inmates who were about to be released, completing resumes for them, teaching them how to interview for jobs, and helping them get substance-abuse treatment on the outside if they needed it. I believe Chris was truly sorry for what he'd done; he still called his wife the love of his life.

Chris wasn't our only player with extensive baseball experience.

Leonard Neal had been drafted by the Los Angeles Dodgers but joined the Marines and then was injured in a car accident. Leonard was in prison for aggravated assault. Steven Washington, who was serving an eleven-year sentence on drug charges, played baseball in college, along with pitcher Tony Gonzalez. Tony was a former model, and his picture was actually on the cover of a devotional Bible I used. It showed him walking on the beach with a couple of children. Tony knew and loved the Lord, but he'd made some bad decisions that sent him to San Quentin.

Our roster of players over the years included a cast of characters, that's for sure. Geno Glaze played third base for us—even though he had only one hand. Marty Valenzuela was one of the fastest players on our team and could run from first base to third on a short blooper. He had only one functioning eye but was still a really good hitter. Larry "Popeye" Faison was a left-handed pitcher from Oakland and played on the team well into his fifties. He learned to play the trumpet and performed the "Star Spangled Banner" before one of our games. Mike Ngo, a Vietnamese-American, didn't know how to catch or throw a baseball when we found him, but he was incredibly strong due to martial arts, and had big hands. He ended up leading our team in homers one season.

We never knew what was going to disrupt our games, which had to be completed before dark (we didn't have lights) and prior to the 8 P.M. inmate count at North Block. Some of our games were disrupted when players' wives arrived for conjugal visits or when family members came to see them. Vinnie Marchesano, an outfielder from New York (we called him "New York"), loved baseball so much that he tried to talk his parents out of coming to see him because he'd miss a game. They hadn't visited him in a couple of years! Eugene Carlisle, who set a team record with thirteen home runs one season, apparently couldn't stay away from the squad. He was released after serving several years for a manslaughter charge, but then broke his parole, returned to San Quentin, and rejoined the team.

How Baseball Helped

I think that the thing I'm most proud of when I reflect on my time coaching the San Quentin Giants is how many of players were released from prison and became productive citizens. Pat Mims became a program director for the Bay Area Women Against Rape (BAWAR) and was recognized by the Federal Bureau of Investigation in 2014 for his work to prevent child sex trafficking. Pat earned a college degree while in prison and turned his life around, and now he's doing really important work to keep children safe. Bryan Smith married Alison Harrington, who, as a seminary student, worked as our scorekeeper and interned at the prison chapel. Alison is a pastor at a church in Tucson, Arizona, and Bryan is sharing his story of redemption to youth groups in an attempt to keep kids out of trouble.

Three of my former players are now working for me. Leonard Neal, German Yambao, and Jason Gottlieb work with Project IMPACT (Incarcerated Men Putting Away Childish Things), a nonprofit group that I'll tell you more about later. Leonard is the chief operating officer of the program. Jason is one of my senior facilitators and works very well with at-risk youth. German was born in the Philippines; his family immigrated to the United States when he was nine years old. His father died in a factory accident less than a month after they arrived in San Francisco. German was convicted of murder when he was eighteen. After spending twenty-five years in prison, German told me that he didn't commit the crime. He'd appeared in front of the parole board several times, admitted to the crime, and expressed remorse. That's what other prisoners told German he had to do to get out.

"I didn't do it," German said. "But if I say I'm innocent, they'll never let me out."

"What do you want to do?" I asked him. "Do you want to keep living a lie until that lie gets you out? Or do you want to tell the truth and live with the truth? It's really up to you. I can't tell you what to do because I'm not going to do the time. You need to pray about it."

German came back to me a few days later and said he was going to tell the parole board the truth. The board denied him parole each of the next two years, but he was released in 2007, after serving twenty-eight years and three months in prison. Today, he works as a facilitator at IMPACT and is a certified substance-abuse counselor.

Frank O'Connell, one of our first basemen, was convicted of murdering a man in Pasadena, California, in 1985. Frank maintained his innocence from the day he arrived at San Quentin, and I believed him after he shared his story with me. I watched Frank and studied his demeanor. He didn't act like a criminal, especially not a murderer, but police accused Frank of shooting and killing twenty-seven-year-old Jay French in the parking garage of an apartment complex on January 5, 1984. Three witnesses told a judge that Frank was with them thirty miles away. Nonetheless, a witness identified Frank as the man who climbed into a car after the shooting, and Frank admitted to having had a short fling with the man's ex-wife several months earlier. He was convicted of murder and a judge sentenced him to twenty-five years to life in prison.

After several years at San Quentin, Frank was able to get Centurion Ministries, a New Jersey–based nonprofit that works to free wrongly convicted prisoners, to investigate his case. The man who was the eyewitness in the parking garage recanted his story and said police pressured him to identify Frank as the shooter. Centurion Ministries' investigators also found three tablets of notes from police detectives that weren't given to Frank's defense attorneys before the trial. The notebooks included evidence that might have exonerated him. A judge overturned Frank's conviction, and he was freed in 2012 after spending twenty-seven years behind bars.

Not all my former players have been freed—and some of them will never get out. Curtis Roberts, one of our shortstops, was arrested in 1994 after stealing two twenty-dollar bills from a liquor store. He was sentenced to a minimum of fifty years in prison with the possibility of parole under California's three-strikes-and-you're-out policy. He'd previously been convicted of stealing seventy-six dollars from a fast-food restaurant and buying twenty dollars' worth of crack. Curtis might have been guilty of being foolish, but he'd never committed a violent crime. He was addicted to drugs and made a few terrible mistakes, but I don't think they were worth his spending the rest of his life in prison.

Curtis isn't eligible for parole until 2044, when he'll be eighty-three years old. I saw Curtis during one of my trips to San Quentin in 2014, and he told me California Governor Jerry Brown wrote him a letter and said he was going to personally review his case. Even though Curtis is facing the possibility of spending most of his life in prison, he still has brightness in him. I hope common sense will one day prevail in his case.

As I look back, I think reintroducing baseball to San Quentin Prison was one of the crowning achievements of my career as chaplain. As I look at the players who got out and became productive citizens, many of whom are making a profound impact on their communities, I have to believe that playing baseball made a difference in their lives. I think it provided them with camaraderie, responsibility, and a sense of pride that they wouldn't have otherwise found inside the walls. For a few hours a couple of days each week, there were no steel bars, handcuffs, or iron gates imprisoning them. They were free to run and have fun together. Not many of my players who were released returned to prison. Nearly all of my former players are out of prison now, and that's the thing that's great. I think that the baseball experiment worked.

RIGHT: Family photo from 1967. Front row: me, Mom, Dad; back row: Betty Jo, Sylvia, Curtis.

Omega Psi Phi Fraternity, Inc.
Mu Gamma Chapter

ABOVE: My dad.

ABOVE: My fraternity picture, 1978. Front row: Irving Fisher and me; back row: David Boyle, Dwight Parker, A.E. Royal, Isaiah Moore, and Willie D. Wilson.

LEFT: Pops and the kids, Earl Jr., Tamara, Ebony, and Franklin.

LEFT: Earl Jr.'s college graduation, Ember Skye, Earl Jr., Jennisys Rene, Angel, and me.

ABOVE: My mother and me.

LEFT: Front row: Pops and Uncle Milbert; second row: Betty Jo and Sylvia; third row: Angel, me, Ebony, Franklin, Tamara, and Earl Jr.

ABOVE: Sylvia, Pops, and Betty Jo.

ABOVE: Angel, Pops, and me.

ABOVE: Sylvia, Mom, and Betty Jo.

ABOVE: Pops's last time on the lake.

ABOVE: IMPACT founders back at San Quentin for an IMPACT graduation: Kevin, Sterling, me, Pat, and Eddie.

ABOVE: The IMPACT Team before release. Front row: Jessie, Leonard, Shahid; back row: Robyn, Bryan, Juan, Don, Kevin, Sterling, and Eddie.

ABOVE: IMPACT class being taught in the California Department of Corrections Division of Juvenile Justice. Jason Gottlieb was the facilitator.

ABOVE: The San Quentin Mass Choir: "He's All I Need."

LEFT: Geronimo Pratt, me, and Bruce White in New Orleans. (Photograph © Michael Zagaris)

RIGHT: The first team built the first field; San Quentin: 9, San Francisco Giants Fantasy Team: 8.

LEFT: Chapel Volunteer Recognition.

RIGHT: National Chaplain of the Year Award: Frank and Bonnie Costantino, me, and Angel.

LEFT: First community graduation for post-crime achievers in Marin City.

ABOVE: Photo from 9/11 Ground Zero: Keena Turner, Junior Bryant, Steve Young, Jesse Sapolu, me, Rodney Knox, and Kirk Reynolds alongside 9/11 rescue workers. (Photograph © Terrell Lloyd)

RIGHT: German Yamboa and Frank O'Connel, both innocent and free.

LEFT: Praying with Moran Norris and Frank Gore before a game. (Photograph © Bill Fox)

ABOVE: The family together before a 49ers game: Anita (Franklin's girlfriend), Franklin, Tamara, Ebony, Earl Jr., Angel, and me.

LEFT: Me, my nephew Kevin Fox, and Dad on the field before a 49ers game.

RIGHT: San Francisco 49ers alumni Eric Wright, Guy McIntyre, Dan Bunz, Dwight Clark, and Dwaine Board with the mentoring team: Archie Gilchrist, Doug Pratt, Andy Mecca, Lee Kooler, and Jim Kooler.

ABOVE: Steve Young and me.

ABOVE: Angel and I visiting Coach John Wooden

ABOVE: Moran Norris, Bryant Young, Jim Brown, me, and Frank Gore. (Photograph © Bill Fox)

ABOVE: The game ball from the Terrell Owens celebration on the Dallas star.

ABOVE: Me, Mel Carriere, and Dad at a San Francisco Giants game.

ABOVE: Dr. Harry Edwards, Coach Walsh, and me.

ABOVE: Me, my brother Curtis, and Dad.

LEFT: Dad with one of his favorite keepsakes, a ball from Terrell Owens.

ABOVE: Golden State Warriors Chapel. Front row: Danny Green (Spurs), Shaun Livingston, David Lee, me, Andre Iguodala, and Justin Holiday; back row: Draymond Green, Steph Curry, and Harrison Barnes.

RIGHT: Prayer after the game.

LEFT: Larry Allen, me, and Bryant Young.

RIGHT: Praying with Kurt Warner after his last professional game.

10

Chess on Thursdays

T HE INFAMOUS SERIAL KILLER CHARLES Manson isn't a very good chess player, but he has an extraordinary mind and a masterful way of influencing people. I learned that by playing chess with him; every Thursday, I played with the inmates. When I did, most of the prison population, men who would normally be at each other's throats, came together with one voice—rooting for me to lose!

As I've said, when I was growing up in Stockton, I was always in trouble. My behavior really bothered my sister Betty Jo, who was a student at Stanford University. I've mentioned how she brought a boyfriend named Freeman home, and she asked him to teach me how to play chess. I think she believed that, if the game occupied my time, it would keep me off the streets. Freeman put a board down between us, set up four rows of black and white pieces, looked at me, and said, "This game is called *chess*."

That day, Freeman patiently showed me how the pieces moved: the rook in a straight line, the bishop diagonally, the queen any which way you wanted her to go, and so on. He explained every rule and didn't repeat himself, as he expected me to pay attention. Freeman told me the game was like war, with moves and counter-moves until one side annihilated the other. I sat motionless for an hour and a half, just listening. Finally, Freeman said, "If you're good at war, you should be good at chess."

Freeman looked at my sister and said, "Let's go." He stood up and they walked out of my parents' house together. I never played a game with Freeman—I'm sure he was good enough that he didn't want to waste his time whipping a novice, but I was hooked on chess from the moment he introduced me to the game. I think that's what my sister wanted to happen. The game challenged my mind, which was apparently hungry for one.

I became obsessed with chess. Back when I was growing up, the daily newspapers would cover chess games (some still do). I devoured the tiny chess columns on the back page every day and followed the moves, trying to anticipate what the opposing players would do

A Strange Oasis

I began going to chess tournaments in town and playing against other guys, slowly improving. My best friend, Frank, and I would play constantly until my father started calling us Fischer and

Spassky, after the great chess masters. It was surreal. In the midst of all my criminal activity—selling drugs, terrorizing rival gangs, brutalizing people, hanging out at all hours in the city's ugliest neighborhoods—we played chess. Our games formed a strange little oasis of order, quiet, and civility in the midst of violent anarchy.

At the time, I was attending Opportunity Classes, which was another name for Alternative School, which is itself a euphemism for "school for the kids who are headed for prison." There, a black teacher named Bob Powell let me and a white student, Randy Trammell, play chess all day. With me playing the black pieces and Randy the white, I gradually grew more adept at the intricacies of the game. I started playing in tournaments and learned the game by being embarrassed by more advanced players. Eventually, I became the guy who was embarrassing everyone else. After I was shot, I went to college in Dallas and continued to play there, beating most of my classmates.

Chess became one of the threads of my life that stretched all the way from my youth as an unbridled street thug to my new life as a minister carrying out God's Word. It was natural that, when I became chaplain at San Quentin Prison, the game would become a part of my ministry there.

Time to Spare = Time to Play

If I told you that prison was a hotbed of competitive chess, you probably would not believe me. Well, it is. Checkers and chess are many inmates' preferred games. To discourage gambling, the prison administration doesn't allow prisoners to play card games. In fact, I suspect some of the best chess players in the country are being held under lock and key. It makes perfect sense. Inmates have an inexhaustible supply of spare hours. When they're not working, eating, showering, praying in chapel, or recreating in the yard, they're in their cells trying to find ways to use up some of that time.

That's why you see such incredible ingenuity and dedication in maximum-security lockups, where prisoners are often in their cells for up to twenty-three hours per day. With all that available time, guys paint and draw, earn law degrees, master musical instruments, write beautiful poetry, and even figure out ways to heat water using two paper clips and an electrical outlet. And those are just a few, out of hundreds of examples.

Another thing they do is play chess. Chess demands many hours of careful play and study. Because the pieces can move only on limited paths and each square on the board has its own coordinates, it can also be played at a distance. That's essential in prison, since two inmates can't pass a chessboard and pieces back and forth between their cells.

Inmates have been playing chess at San Quentin since at least the late nineteenth century, if not much sooner. Peter Claudianos, a Greek immigrant from San Francisco, was sentenced to life in prison after he and his brother bombed the house of a witness who was scheduled to testify in a bribery and corruption trial involving the city's mayor. Claudianos helped form a chess club inside San Quentin, and soon outside clubs went inside the walls to compete against the inmates. Claudianos also corresponded with several chess columnists at metropolitan newspapers around the country. Prisoners were still carrying on the tradition when I was there.

In prison lockup, this is how chess is played: Inmates make

their board and pieces from a piece of paper. They draw numbers on the paper, corresponding to the squares on a chessboard. Then they cut pieces of paper for each of the pieces and number them. The guy an inmate is playing against has the same setup in his cell. They call out their moves to each other: "Number C to twenty!" The pieces were alphabetical characters and the squares were numbered. An inmate might move his paper bishop to that square, and the guy in the other cell does the same thing. You would think, since the two players can't see the other's boards, that there would be cheating. There isn't. Chess is too important. In this, at least, there is honor among thieves.

When I got to San Quentin and heard about the inmates' interest in chess, I started asking who the best player in the prison was. Everyone had a different answer. I heard about Golden, Richie P., and a bunch of other guys. Every racial group had its champion. I had a cousin named Junior who had been in practically every prison in California. Junior was a fantastic chess player. He would handicap himself by taking his queen off the board, and he'd still whip me. I think I managed to beat him only twice.

Bridge Between Races

Even then I was trying to find ways to get past the deep, ugly racial consciousness of the prison. In prison, racism and racial segregation exist in a sort of time warp—in a way that they no longer exist in the United States outside prison walls. We're certainly not a post-racist society on the outside, but only in prison is the racist divide between black, white, and Hispanic so overt, tolerated, and toxic. I saw that one of the responsibilities of my ministry would be to find ways to help inmates of different colors coexist. I thought chess might help ease the racial tensions inside San Quentin, and I was willing to give it a try.

I approached one of the guards at the Adjustment Center, Lieutenant Massey, and asked whether it was okay if I played chess with the inmates. No problem, I was told. So I went to a cell and asked the occupant, a Hispanic guy, if he played chess. His enthusiastic response told me that he did, and he said he'd definitely play me. So we sat with our boards—me outside his cell and he within it— and played our game.

Here's the thing: I had to win. I knew that if I didn't win my first San Quentin match, I'd be seen as a pushover and no one would want to play me. So, I called on all my chess knowledge. We played for a while, calling out our moves through the bars. As the game went along, I noticed something that made my spirit soar: Inmates were yelling our chess moves back and forth to each other. As we made moves, they were relayed throughout the cellblock. Then a white guy shouted, "Hey, a little louder, I can't hear your move!" We began calling out our moves in louder voices, just to satisfy our spectators.

Then my opponent made a questionable move and the entire audience broke into a chorus of boos. I chuckled, but then I realized that the prisoners—Hispanic, black, and white—were booing because the Hispanic inmate wasn't just playing for himself but for all of them. He was a surrogate for every incarcerated man in San Quentin, and I was a surrogate for authority and the world outside. Beating me would be striking a blow against the system that kept them under lock and key. In that moment, my opponent was every inmate, regardless of color. The prisoners were united behind him and against me.

That was fine by me. I wanted somehow to ease the racial tensions; if I had to trick them with chess, I didn't think that the Lord would object. I kept playing, but the inmate wasn't close to my level. Still, I passed up several moves to checkmate in order to prolong the game and draw more inmates into the drama. If you're knowledgeable, chess allows that: you might see checkmate in three moves but wait, knowing you'll still make mate in eight moves. Finally, after drawing it out as long as I could, I checkmated my opponent, thanked him, and left to the cheers and jeers of the cellblock.

I returned the next week and told the inmates that I could play only three games per week: one against a black guy, one against a white guy, and one against a Hispanic. That was the beginning of chess on Thursdays. From then on, every Thursday (the last day of my work week) I would take my makeshift chess boards and pieces and visit each of the cellblocks in turn, looking for guys to play. I would go to South Block on Wednesday. However, Death Row was on South Block, and I couldn't play guys there on a regular basis because I also had my ministry on Death Row. I did not have enough time to do both on the same day. Sometimes, I would play a game, but my routine was to play three games per unit. I did the best I could to accommodate every inmate who had an interest.

During that time, I won most of my games, but I definitely didn't win them all. As I said, there are some great chess players in prison, guys with the native intelligence to understand the game and all the time in the world to study and play it. On occasion, they wiped the floor with me.

I was a very good player, but it was important for me to lose occasionally so that the inmates had hope. There were times when, after the guy's first three or four moves, I knew what he was thinking. I then had to decide not to install a defense that I knew would block his plan, or just go along and see what I could do without using the information I knew would shorten the game. And, oh my, when I lost a game it was like Mardi Gras for the inmates. I would often play in the Adjustment Center, and the way the tiers are set up there, officers have to let you out of the block. Sometimes, if the officers were occupied, I had to wait for them. Well, on those occasions when I lost at chess, if the officer on duty was slow letting me out, the prisoners had a great time riding me. They'd shout, "Loser!" and plenty of other things I won't repeat here. I would always laugh. I had a great time; I enjoyed giving them something to be united by, even if that something was reveling in my defeat.

My chess ministry progressed. Chess is a long, drawn-out game and, while I was playing one of the guys, most of the other prisoners who were within earshot forgot they were enemies. For a few hours, you had fifteen or twenty guys who were not thinking about anything but the game. Black guys, white supremacists, and hard Mexican *vatos* would set aside their stewing racial grudges and honor killings and become part of one team: Beat Smithy. It didn't matter if the guy playing me was a member of the Mexican Mafia. He was playing for the honor of the Black Guerillas two tiers up. Then, when the game was over and I left, they would go back to being enemies again. But in prison, even a brief period of peace is a blessed time.

You Lose: Go to Chapel

I used this same strategy throughout my ministry at San Quentin, finding indirect ways to reach out to the prisoners and turn down the heat on the race war. A few guys figured it out. Once, a prisoner called me over on chess day and said, "I know what you're doing." I nodded. It didn't matter. The way I saw it, most prisoners viewed the chaplain as the person in the chapel. I was supposed to lecture them about Christ and the Word, but that's really not how I see my ministry. I believe in emulating Christ, not just talking about Him. In prison, words whisper; actions shout. I wanted to be the person who was out and about and available.

When I played chess with the inmates, I never had my Bible. I never talked about Scripture. I was present and nonjudgmental. I knew I didn't need to talk—they knew why I was there. This was about getting them to talk about themselves, to open up to me. Until they did that, I could speak about Christ but it would be no more than idle words. It wouldn't change one man's heart.

I played basketball and racquetball with the guys. I had a locker with all my sports stuff. My rule was simple: If I beat them, they had to come to church. On Thursdays, Bishop Green, Rev. Johnny Stein, and I would hit the upper yard to play dominoes. Everyone on the yard knew the rules: If the preachers won, they were going to talk religious stuff and you had to go to church. I made it a game with them. The gospel is more than the Bible; it's about who you are. If I can share the Good News in a way that gets people to the point of understanding what it means to act as Christ in this world, I've done my job.

In this way, over time, as we played chess and baseball and sang in the choir, the guys came to know that they could talk to me about a lot of things, and not just in church. I had no intention of trying to force these guys to develop a relationship with Jesus. So many of these men had spent their lives enduring physical and emotional coercion; the last thing I wanted to do was make them feel spiritually coerced. Hitting someone over the head with the Word doesn't work.

In prison, you're transparent. There's a grapevine. The people confined there are street-smart and cynical; there's no putting on a false persona. The inmates will compare notes on you, and any flaws or acting will come out and destroy your credibility. You have to keep it real. You have to be honest and open and have the patience of Job. Chess, baseball—they were all a means to tell people, *I've come to where you are, and maybe one day you'll come to where I am.*

In a community on the outside, people may see their pastor only on Sundays. In prison, they saw me five days a week. It was an opportunity to effect change that I never would have had on the outside. It meant that I had to be at my best, 100 percent authentic, living like Christ instead of just talking like Him, whenever I walked through those gates.

Memorable Matches

Over my years as the Gary Kasparov (Russian chess grandmaster) of San Quentin, I definitely had some memorable matches. I played inmate Murillo, who was a member of the Mexican Mafia. I knew that he was a gang member, but I did not know his level of involvement. As we played, the moves were called out and, for a change, no one cheered and booed. At some point, I realized this was an unusual competition: It seemed that this guy had been tracking my games. He was playing a King's Indian Defense, which no one in the unit had used. It had been quite a while since I played a game requiring this level of skill. Murillo was prepared!

At some point, it became clear there were major bets on this game. I later found out that guys in other units had bet on it. Even the tier officers seemed interested in the outcome. The games are not on the clock, so the game went a while, and then, suddenly, the inmates realized Murillo had made a tactical error, moving his knight into an attack position, which left him open to penetration. Bad move. The inmates started to scream stuff in Spanish. I pounced on him as his fans jeered him. In a marathon game, a quick move might indicate that the player is onto something and getting close to the prize. More shouts. Cheers. We played it to the endgame; Murillo would not concede. I was a hero to the staff for winning; in fact, the word spread to the other units. Staff came up to me and congratulated me. Big game, lots of pressure. Murillo was one of the most skilled inmates I'd played, but I was still able to take advantage of one of his few mistakes.

A few times, I lost to guys who were far better players than I was. That was okay; when you play guys with superior skills, you learn in defeat. I might lose, but the conversations I had and the education I received made it worthwhile, even if my ego took some big blows over the years.

Once, while playing a prisoner whose name I have forgotten, I made a move and he asked, "Why did you do that?" He then dia-grammed all the moves that would follow and told me where the game was going to go because of the one move I made. He was that good. It was a privilege to play guys who were so skilled.

Other memorable games include playing a member of the Black Guerilla Family. Golden was a master. I played him perhaps ten times, but did not win once. I will also never forget my many games with Robert Alton Harris, the first man to be executed after California reinstated the death penalty in 1977. I played games with Robbie until he made his final walk to the gas chamber in 1992. As I said earlier, I haven't played a game of chess since my last game with Robbie.

Chess with Charlie

As close as I was to Robbie, the one game I'll never forget was with Charles Manson. Not because Charlie was such a good player (he wasn't), but because it gave me an opportunity to observe this extraordinary mind up close. In case you've forgotten the particulars, Manson was an orphaned boy and lifelong criminal who became a self-styled guru in San Francisco, assembling a group of brainwashed youths who became known as the Manson Family.

In August 1969, as part of an attempt to set off what he believed was a coming race war, or Helter Skelter, as he called it, Manson convinced members of his family to murder seven people. On August 9, 1969, Manson told four of his followers to go to a house in Los Angeles and kill the people inside. Actress Sharon Tate and her husband, Hollywood director Roman Polanski, were renting the home. Charles believed a man who had refused to help his fledgling musical career was living there. Manson's followers brutally murdered Tate, her unborn baby, and four others who were visiting her. The next night, Manson's followers murdered Leno and Rosemary LaBianca in their home. Manson and several of his followers were arrested for the murders in December 1969. On March 29, 1971, Manson was sentenced to death. When California repealed the death penalty in 1972, his sentence was reduced to life in prison with the possibility of parole. He is now being held at Corcoran State Prison.

It's certain that Charlie will die in prison. I doubt that he cares too much. In prison, Charlie is a sinister figure of evil, a criminal mastermind, even an icon. He's a celebrity. If he ever gets out, what would he be? What would he do? On the outside, he'd be a bitter old man, quickly forgotten. While there would be people who would follow Charlie, I believe that he would be demented and unable to function outside the structure of a cell.

However, from the depths of San Quentin, Charlie has a mystique. He has a way of reaching people you would not think could be reached. The story is told about an officer who enjoyed making fun of Charlie. He would really get going, and the inmates in the other cells would join in. One day he went home and someone came from behind the bushes and said, "Leave Charlie alone." Charlie's mail and phone calls were monitored, yet he was able to get a message to someone and have the officer followed and confronted at his home.

Some who worked in the prison were transfixed by him; they went out of their way to meet or get close to him. He was *the* Charles Manson, someone they had heard about since childhood, his lean face, burning eyes, and the swastika tattooed into his forehead appearing regularly on television and in newspaper photographs. He has a power over people.

I know a pastor whom Charlie had written regularly. He was a prison volunteer who met Charlie for the first time while he was housed at California Medical Facility. After Charlie arrived at San Quentin, the volunteer asked if he could see Charlie and stated he felt like he was making some progress with him. I allowed him visit Charlie and eventually they started to correspond. I told the pastor, "Don't flinch, be consistent in your responses, don't act as if he is doing you a favor writing to you." I established a rule: the letter had to go to a PO Box (so Charlie wouldn't have his address) and someone from his church had to monitor the incoming and outgoing letters. I warned the pastor, "Charlie will do something to draw attention to himself between now and 2027." That's when his next parole hearing will be—if he lives that long. Charlie loves to show off how he can use his mind to control people. Eventually the time came for me to take my chess game to the unit where Charlie had been transferred—Carson section, first floor, right by the counselor's office. One week, I walked up to his cell and said, "Charlie, it's your turn to play." He turned his wild eyes on me and screamed, "Who says this? It's my world! I tell you when to play!" I shrugged, turned, and walked away. He shouted after me, "Hey, where are you going? Come back here!" I didn't turn back. I kept walking and found three other inmates to play that day.

The following Thursday, I was walking by his cell and he said, "Hey, can we play chess?" He had figured out that he couldn't control me, so I had become interesting. "I'll play you if I have time," I told him as I kept walking. After games with a couple of other inmates, I unfolded my portable stool and sat down opposite Charlie's cell and we started to play. As the match unfolded, I found out that he was one of the most intelligent inmates I'd met in San

Quentin. He talked about himself as the game went on: He had always been a little guy, and that meant that he was often beaten up in the orphanages where he spent most of his time as a boy. He learned to use his mind to fight back. "I had to figure out how to manipulate people's minds and get them to do what I wanted them to do," he told me. Charlie had used that same charisma to manipulate people into committing murder.

Charlie is an average chess player, but his ability to keep his train of thought was incredible. If our game ended in the middle of a conversation, the next time I saw him he would pick up the thread of our conversation at exactly the point at which we left off, even if it was weeks later. Despite this, I beat him whenever we played, though I spun our games out for a while, so that I could learn more about him. I knew I couldn't let him beat me or every time I walked by his cell in the future I would have to hear about it.

He's not Charles Manson, evil incarnate, to me. He's just Charlie, this weird little guy who, even in the midst of being strange and mentally ill, was not as weird as I thought he would be—and probably not as crazy as other people think he must be. Some might say that he is crazy like a fox.

The following story perfectly illustrates Charlie's ability to control people and situations: In 1988, as he was getting ready to do a television interview with Geraldo Rivera, he called me over. He told me, "Just watch." I watched the interview. Charlie was chained to a chair, waving his arms, gesturing wildly in response to Geraldo's questions. Despite their difference in size and the fact there were guards all around them, Geraldo was clearly terrified. But this was a big deal for Geraldo, a career-making interview.

Then, out of nowhere, Charlie growled and lunged at Geraldo, who flipped out and practically tipped his chair over. Charlie just cackled while the guards subdued him. Later in the interview, Charlie threatened to behead Geraldo. Charlie was led away in a big scene. After that, Charlie started getting letters of support at the prison, some even containing money orders. Charlie set the thing up just to show everyone that, even while manacled and surrounded by guards, he could manipulate people. Geraldo was a pawn to him, just like the pieces on the chessboard.

Creative for Christ

For me, chess was an example of the limitless ways in which God is able to bless others. When you are trying to bring people to Jesus in an environment that is so averse to trust, talk is cheap. You have to be willing to think outside the box and find creative ways of demonstrating Christ within yourself. You have to build trust and show the people you're dealing with that you are living the Word that you are sharing with them. It can't be an act. Playing chess allowed us to get acquainted from a different perspective. I was just a guy who happened to like some of the things that were important to them and, by the way, I was the chaplain.

Men and women fail all the time, but if that trust is built in Jesus, it lasts. I've seen men I played chess with many years ago in prison who are still walking with the Lord. I believe that to reach its fullest expression, ministry has to exceed outside the walls of the church or the prison. God has blessed a lot of us with tools and gifts, many of which lie outside the boundaries of what we think of as traditional ministry. But to me, when you're attempting to reach souls lost in isolation and anger, all's fair game. You can't limit yourself. If you do, you limit God. But if you use the tools you have and think creatively, you expand God's presence.

For me, chess was one of those tools. I never expected that it would become so significant, many years after my sister's boyfriend introduced me to the game. But God did.

11

San Quentin Choir

W<small>HEN</small> I <small>BECAME THE CHAPLAIN</small> at San Quentin Prison, no choir existed. Only four or five inmates attended chapel regularly, so I went searching for ways to get more guys to come to my services. Along with playing chess and baseball and participating in other activities with the inmates, I realized music might be one way to draw guys into the chapel.

I've always believed that part of the church experience must involve music. Music can change a person's mood, enhance one's memories, act as a carrier for suggestions, and even influence the mind. In a prison, music can also serve as a form of therapy: It can help alleviate an inmate's stress or pain and allow him to more easily express his feelings. Even though I'm not a musician or singer, I believe music reaches certain people in ways that words sometimes can't. Just imagine watching your favorite movie without any music. It wouldn't be the same!

Shortly after I arrived at the prison, I set out to find a handful of singers and musicians to help spread God's Word inside the walls of San Quentin. Fortunately, I met Hampton Finney early in my tenure as chaplain. Finney, who is from Los Angeles, had worked with his church choir before he became an inmate at San Quentin. Finney was very instrumental in helping me get the chapel choir started. He went through the blocks of San Quentin listening for the best voices and, when he found a singer, he was very persuasive in getting him to give gospel music a try.

Our first choir was a quintet: Ronnie Ross, Lamont Williams, Jessie Reed, Benny "Shorty P" Parks, and Darrell "Big D" Wright. Ronnie and I had grown up in Stockton together. Ironically, Ronnie was shot the same night I was shot in a different part of town, and he was one of the guys who came to ask if I wanted them to kill the guys who shot me. After I was saved and moved to Dallas, Ronnie shot and killed an undercover narcotics officer.

"Big D" was one of the most respected inmates at San Quentin. As Darrell's moniker suggests, he was a large man and, at one time, had bench-pressed more weight than any other inmate in the California prison system. Darrell was a mountain of a man, but he also had a very beautiful and powerful voice.

Ronnie, Darrell, and the others were rhythm-and-blues singers inside the prison, and many of the inmates started coming to church to hear the guys sing. Hampton directed the quintet and found a few musicians to supply the background music. We called the group the Chapel Tones and they became our first choir.

Gospel Fest

On one occasion, Terrance Kelly, a renowned music director, called my office and said that he and the Oakland Interfaith Choir wanted to come and minister at San Quentin. As a result of that evening, we were blessed to have Terrance Kelly request to be a chapel volunteer. He assisted the choir and entered our group in the Bay Area McDonald's Gospel Fest. Terrance was able to persuade the judges to accept a video of the choir in place of a live performance.

After some months of preparation, with six-foot-six, 380-pound Pone "Zero" Uperesa as the choir director and local television station KTVU doing the taping, the recording was entered in the competition. Nathaniel Lane, who had a voice like Sam Cooke, led a song titled "I Am Not the Same." The performance is widely viewed as one of the best songs ever to come from our ministry. Entering the Gospel Fest gave the community a new awareness of what Christ was doing behind the walls of San Quentin.

Over time, more guys joined the choir and it became bigger and bigger. Derrick Duncan, from Oakland, and Leonard Brown were among the first singers to join the quintet, then we were really blessed when the Lord brought us two women from outside the prison who took our choir to new heights. Arvis Strickling-Jones, who has been playing gospel music since age seven, was the minister of music at St. Stephen Baptist Church in San Francisco. She has recorded five gospel albums and performed around the globe. She's a world-class gospel singer and she didn't live far from San Quentin Prison. Arvis served as a volunteer musical director for our choir, and with her help our group performed her song, "A Friend," on ABC's *Good Morning America*.

Carolyn Anderson was another top church choir director in the Bay Area. She volunteered at San Quentin as a voice coach and piano player. I know that our choir would have never got off the ground without Carolyn and Arvis's help.

He's All I Need

I've learned many times during my life that God is in control of everything, and I'm confident that it was His work that led to my chapel choir recording a CD in 1992. I don't believe it was fate or luck; it was the will of God. Whatever outcome He desires will come to pass. For reasons only God knows, he brought my chapel choir together with a group of Buddhist monks and members of the Grateful Dead, the psychedelic rock-and-roll band that had toured the world for three decades. Together, we completed a project that I'm sure no one at San Quentin—or outside the prison walls— would have ever envisioned.

The Monks

In December 1988, Grateful Dead drummer Mickey Hart arranged for the Gyuto Tantric Choir to come to the United States so he could record their traditional polyphonic chanting. Hart was working with archivists at the Library of Congress and the Smithsonian Institution to record global musical traditions that were on the verge of extinction. Hart recorded sounds from all over the world, including New Guinea tribesmen and an all-female Latvian choir,

but it was the Gyuto monks' low, guttural chanting that mesmer-
ized him.

Gyuto is one of the monastic institutions of the Gelug Order,
which has been around since AD 779, when Buddhism was the
state religion of Tibet. The Gyuto monks opened a university in
Tibet in 1474, just a few years before Christopher Columbus discovered the New World. For nearly five hundred years, they lived
very peaceful and isolated lives there. But after the Chinese invaded
Tibet in 1950, the Gyuto monks were exiled, along with His Holi-
ness the Fourteenth Dalai Lama. About sixty monks fled to India,
where they reestablished a monastery in Tenzing Gang in
Arunachal Pradesh. Today, the main Gyuto monastery is located
near Dharamsala, India, with about five hundred monks in the
order.

The Gyuto monks are perhaps best known for their traditional
chants, which are a form of meditation and spiritual development.
The transcendent chants are sacred offerings to Tibetan Buddhist
deities and enlightened beings, and are rarely heard outside the
monastery's walls. Sometimes, the monks use instruments such as
delicate cymbal taps and long alpenhorn-like instruments (similar
to the long horns people in the Swiss mountains play), which are
supposed to represent the distinct calls of one male and one female
elephant. Collectively, the harmony produces a unique and beautiful sound.

Twenty-one Gyuto monks came to the United States to record
an album with Mickey. While the monks were performing in the
Bay Area, Danny Rifkin, the Grateful Dead's manager, was driving
them in a van over the San Rafael Bridge. When they drove past
San Quentin, the monks suddenly started shouting, "Trapped souls!

Trapped souls!" The monks didn't even know San Quentin was a prison. Danny drove them to a road near the gates. Right there on the shoulder, the monks performed their traditional puja, in which they bowed, prayed, and collectively chanted to free the enslaved spirits and souls of the inmates. I'm sure it was a sight to see for any people who drove by.

Three years later, the Gyuto Tantric Choir returned to the United States for a concert tour. Danny called and said he wanted to bring the monks into the prison. I told him that the monks were welcome to come to the chapel. After I told some of the inmates about the monks' visit, they were skeptical, to say the least. Inmates who had come to accept Jesus Christ as their Lord and Savior were concerned that the monks were going to try to brainwash them into accepting Buddha. I told the prisoners to pray about it. I told them I believed it would be an enriching experience for them and would be an opportunity to share God's Word. "Sometimes, the Lord wants us to see the plight of others," I told them.

I was delighted that the inmates chose to open our chapel and their hearts to the monks. However, when Danny showed up in January 1992 with an entourage of strange-looking people, including the hippie entertainer Wavy Gravy, who wears a propeller on his colorful hat, and Ram Dass (Richard Alpert), who was famous for his research work with Timothy Leary at Harvard University about the potentially therapeutic effects of hallucinogenic drugs, the inmates didn't want anything to do with them. I think they believed, as Christians, that they couldn't have Buddhists in the church. I invited the monks and everyone else to come to the chapel, but the members of my choir refused to minister to them.

Then, in the church, the monks began chanting, and the halls around the prison filled with an extraordinary harmony. The monks' distinct chords and tones echoed off the prison walls, and it was a sound never before heard inside San Quentin. The sounds moved the guys in my choir, and they decided to return the honor by singing for the monks. My choir sang "Amazing Grace." I think it deeply touched Danny and the others in their group that an inspiring harmony could be produced in such a dark and lonely place. I also think that the inmates learned they had more in common with the monks than they believed. Like the inmates, the monks had been enslaved and outcast by society. These peaceful, spiritual people were enslaved, murdered, and persecuted for their religious beliefs. They were driven from their homeland by the Chinese government. I think many of my inmates could sympathize with what the monks had endured.

Getting Ready

When Danny left the prison, the group went to the Rex Foundation, the nonprofit charity of the Grateful Dead family, and told them they wanted to record an album with my choir. Cameron Sears from the Rex Foundation contacted me a few weeks later and told me what Mickey wanted to do. I told them my choir would do it, but only on the condition that I could have female prison-staff members sing to balance the men in the choir. I went to Warden Daniel Vasquez and asked for permission to record an album with female staff members performing as well. Once again, Warden Vasquez recognized the benefits of the project and gave me permission to move forward. It was the first time in the United States that prison staff and inmates would sing together on a musical CD. They became the San Quentin Mass Choir.

Danny and Mickey told me that my choir would have to work very hard during the next few months, which could be a problem as an execution was approaching. Part of the execution protocol was curtailing inmate movement. There were certain days when evening movement was cancelled. Although they were impressed by the wonderful sounds they heard in the chapel, Danny and Mickey told me my guys' voices were pretty raw and unrefined. Mickey said they would have to practice every day for two months before he would record them.

With the help of Carolyn Anderson, choir director Mandell Motley, and producer Donald Cronk, Mickey worked to raise our choir to a professional level. We ended up having four female guards—Velda Dobson, Toni Marshall, Versie McGee, and Angel Schramm—sing in our choir. Each of the female guards sang a solo track on the album. There were ten other ladies from the prison's records department, warehouse, and hospital who sang in the choir, too. The music wouldn't have sounded right without those ladies' beautiful voices.

A few of my guys were exceptionally talented singers and sang lead vocals on the album. Roderick Boddie had an unbelievable voice and a genuine sensitivity for old-school gospel music. Ronald Williams, who was released from prison shortly after we completed the album, sang lead on three of the nine tracks. We also had volunteers who sang on the album. John Cooks and Anthony Lee, who were members of my church, and Bertha Howard blessed us with their powerful voices. Coming into the prison and helping with the choir was their ministry. Over time, the chapel choir became a success, because people from the community invested their time to help the inmates become stronger in their faith, as well as in their musical talents.

The Band

We also had some very talented musicians. C. T. Jones, an officer at the prison, played the organ, Bill McMullen, another lieutenant, played the drums, and Counselor Herbert Hammond read Bible passages during one of the songs. Eugene Johnson played rhythm guitar and openly wept while playing because he was so overcome by the music. Terry Thomas was a talented left-handed guitarist, Ruben Sanchez was a drummer, Randy Yates played the piano, and Isaac Whitworth was a keyboardist. Luke Oliver, a bass guitarist, was the oldest inmate in the choir. We called him Cool Hand Luke, because he played so well.

Mike Etchison was our harmonica player. When I met Mike for the first time, he had hair down to his rear and was wearing biker boots. He was still a very rebellious man. After I baptized Mike, he cut his hair and became a model prisoner.

Mike was a fantastic musician. When blues musician Norton Buffalo performed at San Quentin one time, Mike played harmonica for him. Norton was so impressed that he gave Mike a box of harmonicas after his concert. Mike was released from prison in 2006 and is doing very well on the outside.

The Album

Finally, after a couple of months of practice, Mickey and Danny showed up at San Quentin on May 9, 1992, with the Grateful Dead's mobile recording unit, which was the same system used to record hundreds of the band's live concerts. It was only a few weeks after Robert Alton Harris was executed, so there was still a lot of tension inside the prison walls. In a couple of hours, our chapel was transformed into a recording studio. With Mickey and Mandell Motley directing the choir, we recorded an album of ten songs in about fourteen hours. The CD included "I'm on the Lord's Side," "He Watches Over Me," and "You Can Make It If You Try."

Some weeks after the recording, Mickey realized some things needed to be corrected and, with the warden's permission, C. T. Jones, Herbert Hammond, Angel Schramm, and Bill McMullen escorted Ronald Williams, Mandell Motley, and Johnny Powell to the Grateful Dead's Fantasy Records studio in San Francisco to put the finishing touches on the project. The album was entitled *He's All I Need*.

He's All I Need garnered a lot of international attention, because it was the first musical collaboration between inmates and prison guards. Plus, I like to think people were really drawn to the inspirational message of our music and the performers' talent. The album climbed to number thirty-nine on Billboard's gospel charts, and the project was featured in *People* magazine, as well as on CNN and other networks. We sold thousands of copies around the world. The money from the sales of the CDs went to a victim relief fund, to support children we adopted through World Vision, a relief organization, and to provide scholarships for children we deemed deserving, as well as to the Garden Chapel (the prison church) and other projects. We used some of the money to purchase musical equipment and to fix up the chapel. We turned it into the finest chapel in the prison system.

More important, the album brought the inmates and prison guards together. Correctional officers and other staff members started coming to chapel service, and several of them brought their families to our Easter banquet. That was the most gratifying part of the project for me. I've always believed that, as chaplain, one of my most important duties was to break down barriers inside the prison. One of the biggest barriers I wanted to topple was between the inmates and guards. Society believes inmates and correctional officers are supposed to be adversaries, but we showed the outside world that even people who have differences are able to come together with a common thread, which is the gospel of Jesus Christ. We used our music as a pipeline to deliver our message to the outside world.

The chapel choir helped a lot of the San Quentin inmates turn their lives around. You can go down the list of singers and musicians, and nearly all of them are out of prison and continuing the ministry. Hampton Finney is a bishop with a church in Los Angeles, and Mandell Motley is a pastor of a church in Martinsville, Virginia. I believe that the chapel choir taught them consistency of character and responsibility to the Word. If you were part of the choir, you had to adhere to the same set of rules I had for playing on the baseball team: you couldn't sing in the choir if you didn't behave on your cellblock, didn't go to work, and didn't come to chapel services. I think the rules and values in the choir helped shape their lives.

Looking back, I think *He's All I Need* proved to a lot of people that anything is possible, even inside a desolate place like San Quentin Prison. For a couple of months, fifty people came together to produce something beautiful, inspirational, and powerful.

12

Forgiveness

DURING MY YEARS AT SAN Quentin Prison, I came across dozens of characters, both good and bad. I met guys who had been in my gangs back in Stockton and guys from rival gangs. I met white supremacists, devil worshippers, Wiccans, and some people who were truly innocent of the crimes that sent them to prison. The inmates at San Quentin came from all types of places and socioeconomic backgrounds. There were white- and blue-collar criminals, rapists, murderers, gang bangers, and thieves. There were white guys, black guys, Latinos, Pacific Islanders, and other races. Many of them had one thing in common, though: they called me Chap or Smithy.

One such inmate was Blue Jordan, who during my tenure at San Quentin was transferred to a minimum-security ranch. Well, Blue learned that his wife became romantically involved with another guy while he was being held behind bars. One night, Blue escaped from the ranch and an ex-inmate picked him up. They made their way to Blue's house, knocked on the door, then beat the daylights out of the guy. Then Blue raced back to the ranch and by the time the guards came to his dormitory that night, he was back lying on his bed. They told him, "Blue, we have you as an escapee." But Blue was in his bunk and the guards had no witnesses. So Blue beat down the man that was messing with his wife and got away with it. That's hard core.

Charles "Cool Pop" Giles was an inmate at San Quentin and was also one of my distant cousins. At one time, he actually lived in the house where I was shot. Charles was a heroin addict and was in and out of jail. When I was chaplain, Charles was getting ready to parole and came to my office.

"Hey, cuz, I need you to do something for me," he said.

"What do you need?" I said.

"I need you to hold my TV until I come back," he said.

Even though Charles was being paroled, he was convinced he wouldn't stay out of prison. One time, some of his cousins picked him up from Deuel Vocational Institution (DVI) after he was paroled and decided they were going to let him smoke crack. Charles had never smoked crack before. He tried it and jumped out of the car because he thought his hair was on fire. "Don't ever give me that stuff again," he said. Then he was caught stealing a carton of cigarettes and was arrested. He was sentenced under Proposition 184, the so-called three-strikes law, and given a sentence of twenty-five years to life. He was sent to Folsom State Prison, where he didn't have a television.

Another inmate I became close to was Michael Thompson, the

leader of the Aryan Brotherhood. You might wonder how a white supremacist became close friends with an African-American chaplain, but Michael and I seemed to hit it off from the start. About a year after I started working to try to bridge the racial divide in the prison, Michael quit the Aryan Brotherhood because they'd killed a young kid. One night, I received an emergency telephone call at home. A correctional officer told me I needed to come back to the prison because Michael had a knife in the hospital and would talk only to me.

I rushed back to San Quentin and officers escorted me to a secure area. When Michael surrendered, he gave me a piece of paper with a phone number written on it. He told me to notify the woman on the other end that she was in danger of being killed and needed to leave her home immediately. He saved the woman's life. Michael had become an informant against the Aryan Brotherhood, and many people he'd talked about were now in real danger. To this day, Michael is in protective custody because the Aryan Brotherhood has a standing hit on him.

The Value of Forgiveness

I've mentioned that my experiences in San Quentin taught me many valuable lessons. Even in such a dark and isolated place, I found so many examples of redemption, kindness, love, patience, courage, compassion, generosity, joy, and yes, even humor. However, I think the primary thing I learned during my tenure was the value of forgiveness.

There was an inmate, Michael T, who was an early recruit and member of the Aryan Brotherhood. Michael had done a number of stretches in prison dating back to the1970s and was proud of his Aryan commitment. One day, while reading *Where Flies Don't Land*, a book written by Jerry Graham about his experiences while incarcerated at San Quentin, something happened to Michael's racist heart and all the anger, bitterness, and hatred he harbored.

Michael was paroled and later arrested on new charges. I heard about this guy who was covered in shamrocks, lightning bolts, and Nazi signs who was walking the yard and trying to talk to men about Jesus. I finally met him—it was Michael T—and he shared what happened when he read that book. The look in Michael's eyes and my heart told me this guy truly wanted to serve the Lord. I told him I wanted him to come and work for me in the chapel.

You can imagine what some of the chapel brotherhood thought of my bringing in Michael. When he came to work for me, he asked if he could be in charge of cleaning the bathrooms. He said he wanted to work where no one else wanted to and to serve God by cleaning other men's messes. Michael had the toilets shining, the sinks sparkling, and the floor glowing. In fact, one guy slipped on the floor because it was waxed so well! Michael took pride in being a janitor for the Lord.

He was from the South, and he had endured a very rough upbringing. Michael said he was not a hillbilly, he was a hillwilliam. He had done things for the Aryan Brotherhood that he was ashamed of. A major part of his becoming a drug addict stemmed from his guilt over what he'd done.

As Michael started to grow, he sang in the worship service. The guys in the chapel began to treat him with love, and his heart melted even more. Michael found acceptance and forgiveness from some of the same guys he would have once tried to kill. Upon his release, Michael T started Jordan Crossings, a church and ministry to house and nurture men recently released from prison who wanted to live lives of forgiveness and freedom.

The Power of Unforgiveness

I told you how I learned the power of forgiveness early in my career as chaplain, as soon as I confronted the man who shot me, in his cell. God wanted me to face the person who had wounded me—literally—and left me carrying a burden of anger and resentment for years. Even though I had walked the path of ministry and had done my best to put that trauma behind me, it still had a hold on my soul.

When you cannot forgive, you give life to whatever harmed you in the past. It's not a conscious decision. No matter how much you insist that you are over it, the hidden rage, fear, and desire for revenge will stalk you and cast a shadow over every part of your life. The hunger for vengeance can be all-consuming.

I've seen this in some of the families of murder victims who spend years advocating for the killers of their loved ones to be executed. Finally, the anticipated date with the gas chamber arrives and, after it's all over, they don't find the peace or closure that they thought they would. The love they had for their family member or close friend became hatred and loss. That is a tragedy almost as terrible as the death of the victim: the blighting of the survivors' lives by fury and the white-hot need to inflict retribution.

In His wisdom, God knows this. That's why He created us with the capacity to forgive, surely one of the most divine aspects of humanity. No other creature has the power to consciously regard another being and say, "You injured me, and I forgive you." If lack of forgiveness is a form of bondage, then mercy is release. You can't move on with your life until you forgive.

Keep in mind that I am not calling for excusing crimes. God is a God of mercy, but He is also a God of justice. Forgiving someone does not cancel his offense, nor does it absolve him of responsibility. In my time at San Quentin, I witnessed several instances when the families of murder victims wrote letters to men on Death Row, saying that they forgave them, but still thought they should die for their deeds. Forgiveness is not about the person you are forgiving; it's about setting yourself free.

The Primal Drive

I understand the primal drive for vengeance. It's a very human need, but it's indicative of our most primitive nature, a reflection of our fallen state. Mercy, empathy, and compassion are part of our higher selves, how we reflect God. When we let go of our hardened anger to forgive someone, we are acting more like God. If lack of forgiveness holds us in bondage (sometimes for years), it's the release of forgiveness that allows us to move forward on new paths in our lives.

Now, some people might argue, "Why should someone who has committed a terrible crime get the gift of forgiveness? They should have to suffer with the guilt of what they've done." One of the most pervasive ideas about forgiveness is that it's weak. If you hold onto resentment and the desire for revenge, most of our so-

ciety believes that you're being strong; the opposite is actually
true.

First of all, exactly how does refusing to forgive someone make
you stronger? In reality, holding onto the desire for revenge might
make you obsess about causing pain to another, make you feel im-
potent, prevent you from moving on with your life, and cause you
to take pleasure in another's misfortune. Worst of all, those things
distance you from God.

The refusal to forgive and the thirst for vengeance can lead
people to make terrible decisions that ruin their lives. Think of
blood feuds and gang reprisals, murderous choices that are based
on nothing more than the misbegotten idea that an "eye for an eye"
means justice. In truth, as Mahatma Gandhi said so wisely, "An eye
for an eye leaves the whole world blind." [1]

The desire for retribution can come to dominate a person's
thinking until it's all he or she thinks about.

Practicing the Power

Simply put, there is nothing about the refusal to forgive that makes
you stronger. I tried to teach inmates that it only weakens you and
imprisons you behind bars of your own making. In contrast, mercy
and forgiveness are signs of spiritual and moral strength. Think
about it: When you forgive someone, you are exercising grace in the
same way that God does. Grace is unearned favor, and in the same
way that we are humbled by God's unearned favor toward us, your
unearned forgiveness of another person humbles him. In an instant,
you have put him in your debt.

Forgiveness is a powerful act, and this is why mercy is one of the greatest sources of God's power. In granting us forgiveness for our sins, God gives us an undeserved gift, reminding us that we are flawed. In forgiving, the Granter of mercy takes the power away from the person who committed the crime.

The people in South Africa know this well. After the end of apartheid, many black Africans were hungry—understandably—for revenge against the whites who had oppressed and murdered them for generations. But the government had learned the eye-for-an-eye lesson and set up the Truth and Reconciliation Commission, saying that anyone who came forward, confessed his crime, and expressed honest remorse would not be prosecuted. The key was this: The victims had the power to inflict retribution but chose not to use it.

The Truth and Reconciliation Commission outraged many people around the world, but it was a brilliant move to heal a divided country. The government administrators knew that revenge would only lead to more violence. However, forgiveness gave the injured moral standing and authority over their oppressors and allowed South Africa to heal. The victims were given permission to move on with their lives. Their retribution was saying, "I forgive you."[2]

We must always remember to ask the question, *Why do we forgive?* Is the point to let the offender off the hook? No. It is to allow the offended to throw off the chains of resentment and anger and move on. That is the goal we must keep in mind.

Forgiveness Lite

For Christians, forgiveness is the core of our faith, but we tend to get by with what I call forgiveness lite. We ask God to forgive our sins, but what are we really asking for? I tend to believe that we are asking for a shortcut—for God to handle the heavy lifting and do the thing that is hardest for all of us to do: forgive ourselves.

We are our own harshest critics and worst enemies. At San Quentin we had an inmate named Jeffery, whom Terry, Pat, John, and the guys in the leadership group were very concerned about. He would describe hearing voices and became combative to the men who prayed and represented the gospel. He was mean and angry, yet he cried a lot and seemed emotionally troubled. Jeffery felt that he had no redemptive value. He was a murderer, and believed that his life was a waste. Jeffery showed up to work one day and the guys saw a scary change in him. They felt he seemed demon possessed. The following Sunday, they shared the story with me, and asked what we could do to help him. They wanted to know if they could bring him to the chapel, so that I could pray with him.

They brought Jeffery to my office and I could tell he was fighting something within himself. First I just talked with him, while the guys sat quietly praying. I heard a bit of his story: Outside, when he was on drugs, he'd used a baseball bat to kill a man. He knew the Word of God and felt that he was doomed to hell, and had given himself over to Satan.

I asked if I could pray with him. Jeffery said yes, but that it would not matter. The guys who had been praying without ceasing while I talked with him came and joined hands. As we prayed, Jeffery started to shake and went into a trancelike state. We kept praying, the guys were crying, pleading with God to do something and help this troubled man.

Then, a calmness and peace came over the room. Jeffery looked at the guys and said, "I'm fine." Terry and John led him through the gospel anew. After hearing the gospel, he asked to be baptized. Jeffery went on to become a graduate of Biblical Counseling Foundation and, upon his release from prison, he became a church elder and missions pastor. In a place where men are not supposed to care about anything, the guys in the leadership group saw someone who needed help.

Jeffery related that his freedom came when he realized that he could forgive himself for what he had done and that God could still love him. The road that Jeffery is on today, and the lives he has affected for good, may never have happened if not for some guys who believed in the power of forgiveness and prayer.

Forgiving Yourself

Even the most devout Christians, while they might easily forgive others for offenses, are often unforgiving about their own mistakes. This can inhibit their ability to choose the righteous path, because, if they cannot forgive past poor choices, they might come to believe, as Jeffery did, that they supposedly deserve to be on the unsatisfying path that they're on today. If a person can't forgive himself, unhappiness becomes his self-imposed punishment for living an unrighteous life.

Was I punishing myself for my criminal youth by not forgiving Ace, the guy who shot me? I don't know, but it's possible. I do know this: When I thanked him for shooting me, I took back my power. But more important, I felt free. In absolving Ace of his offense, I also absolved myself of my own past mistakes. The only thing that mattered was moving forward on the righteous path, and I prayed that Ace would find his own way through.

We often strike out at what we hate, but we're really striking at something we hate in ourselves. When we refuse to forgive ourselves for our transgressions, we're really punishing that part of ourselves that we hate. In asking God to forgive us for something we haven't forgiven ourselves for, we're only getting half a blessing. God is a just God and He will reward prayers and honest remorse by granting forgiveness for the most grievous actions, but He cannot make us forgive ourselves. At some point, I told inmates, we have to take responsibility for the choices that led us down the wrong path and ask some hard questions: *Am I the same person I was when I made that choice? Do I really want forgiveness? What purpose am I serving by refusing to forgive myself?*

Kevin H.

One of the most poignant examples of self-forgiveness came while I was ministering to an inmate named Kevin H. He had been sent to San Quentin for raping a young girl, and I worked with him for months trying to get him to accept God. I noticed that whenever I worked with Kevin, a female guard would watch us like a hawk. I didn't find out why until later.

One day, Kevin told me that he had decided to accept Jesus Christ as his Savior and would like to be baptized. To do that, he needed to go to the chapel, and the female guard told me that she would escort him to the chapel for the baptism ceremony. I agreed. When I got to the chapel, Kevin and the guard were already there, and as I began the baptism, Kevin mentioned a hymn he wanted to sing, but he didn't know the words. The guard said that she knew them and began singing the hymn as I baptized Kevin. While this was going on, I saw that tears were running down the guard's cheeks.

Later, with the ceremony over and Kevin back in his cell, I asked the guard to come to my office. I asked why she wept. To my astonishment, she told me that Kevin was in prison for raping her daughter! She said that she had specifically requested a transfer to San Quentin so that she would have a chance to kill him. She worked on the gun rail and had the opportunity to fabricate a reason to fire a round as he left his cell to shower or go to the yard.

But in seeing Kevin accept Christ, and then in singing the hymn, she suddenly realized that she needed to forgive him. The hatred she had been harboring in her heart had become too much for her to endure, and she realized she needed to let it go. I believe that in doing so, she also forgave herself for allowing harm to come to her daughter. She gained peace in her heart to move on with her life and to help her daughter to do the same.

That's a stunning act of mercy, but it's something we're all capable of. The spark of the divine in us makes us capable of such acts. If we are to choose better paths, we must remember that forgiveness is a process. We must forgive others, forgive ourselves, and ask God for His forgiveness as well.

You Are Not Your Crime

Mandell was a young man sentenced for fraud. He was from the East Coast and got into trouble trying to fit in and provide for himself and his wife. When he arrived in the prison, I met him and learned his mother was a pastor and that he had grown up in the church. It was clear that he had established some level of relationship with Jesus, yet that relationship was shallow. Many men knew the Word, yet the sad thing was that they had not become intimate with the Word.

After talking with Mandell's family, I realized that I needed to work with him on the meaning of the Christ relationship. As we got into the Bible and started to address issues in his life, he came to a clear realization and stated that what he had done was not who he was. I told him, "Time will tell who you really are."

When Mandell got out of prison, he went back East to help his mother in the church. Time has spoken, and Mandell is not his crime; he is a leading pastor in his denomination. He is doing a great job in ministry!

In working with inmates, one of the key questions I tried to get them to ask was: *Am I my crime?* In other words, did a murderer's or rapist's or thief's past actions define who he was, or was he something more and better? Our society is unforgiving, which is why the United States has the highest incarceration rate of any country in the Western world.[3] Young men who commit crimes are constantly told that they are less than everyone else. Recidivism rates are sky high[4] in part because society penalizes people even after they have paid their debts via the courts and prisons. Some states deny ex-cons the right to vote, while many states force them into years-long probationary and parole periods with little support to get jobs or find stable homes. It's no wonder that many can't forgive themselves when the world around them is constantly finding them guilty.

Even if you think someone is his crime, God does not. He knows better. God doesn't have a checklist for forgiving us for our errors. He cares about only one thing: that we ask Him sincerely for forgiveness through a relationship with Jesus Christ.

Now, keep in mind that even if you do that and God washes you clean of your sins, you still have to pay an earthly price. I know of men on Death Row who asked and received God's forgiveness and were still executed. But where did they go after they died?

I taught inmates that in the eyes of God, they were not their crimes. But they had to believe that. They had to let go of guilt and self-recrimination. They had to grasp that, as reflections of God, they had the potential for good that was far greater than their potential for wrongdoing. I told them, "You are worthy of forgiveness and when you accept that, God's forgiveness can fill your spirit." Loving the Lord isn't enough; I had inmates who loved God but didn't believe, deep down, that they deserved to be forgiven for what they had done. Accepting that they were deserving of God's love and mercy opened the door.

God is a God of today and tomorrow. That's why we go to Him for our future hope. In the end, it comes down to a simple question: Do we trust God? Do we trust Him enough to lay our burdens on Him and allow Him to carry them for us? Vengeance and guilt are two of those burdens.

The Forgiveness of a Child

Forgiveness has a childlike simplicity to it. Several years ago, a friend asked me to preach with him during a five-day revival. He wanted me to preach at Baptist, Methodist, Lutheran, Episcopal, and Catholic churches. As the week went on, I began to question why God wanted me to preach to so many denominations. After I finished at a Catholic church on the final night of the revival, a young girl approached me. She asked me if I knew a particular inmate. "You have to know him," she said. "He's at your prison. Tell him I forgive him."

"Okay, baby," I said, not knowing what the man had done to her.

After the young girl walked away from me smiling, her mother approached me. "What did my little girl tell you?" she asked.

"She told me to tell an inmate that she forgave him," I said.

The girl's mother starting crying, and told me that the man was the little girl's former soccer coach, who had molested her and several other young girls on her team. Her mother told me that the girl had never spoken of the man or his crime.

The next Monday, I located the man at San Quentin. I did not have a relationship with him, but I felt compelled to find him because of the little girl. When I told him why I was there, he started to cry. Based on his tears, I felt the thing he could and should do was to bring some relief to that young girl. I told him, "You're going to write her a letter and tell her that she didn't do anything wrong. Tell her you're sorry for what you've done."

Had he not written the letter, he would have had to carry his guilt. I just felt that it was the right thing to do. Sometimes, as a chaplain, you make choices that you hope will bring positive results. I do not know if that effort changed this inmate; after being processed and evaluated, he was transferred. I do know there is something healing about admitting your faults. This one act at least offered the potential for future healing. He harmed the girl, yet she wanted him to know that she forgave him. Those words had to find a home in the recesses of his being.

When I went to the man's cell the next day, he was crying as he handed me the letter. I read the letter and sent it to her mother. I knew that there was going to be a day when the little girl would need to read it. I didn't know why I had been asked to preach at the revival, but God wanted me to find that little girl. That's divine forgiveness coming from the heart of a child. She kept it simple and, in doing so, showed more wisdom than a thousand adults I've known.

Forgiveness Is Healthy

Forgiveness is the gift that rewards the giver. Only when you can set down the burden of your own guilt and your anger toward others who have wronged you, can you move on down the righteous path. One of my most difficult and emotionally draining duties as chaplain at San Quentin was dealing with families waiting for a criminal to be executed. The experience of holding onto hate and pain for years was often devastating to these people. Lack of forgiveness does something to you. Every time the condemned came up for review, the family would have to go back and relive the horrible crimes that took their loved ones from them. One lady I worked with lost her son, a police officer killed in the line of duty. She wanted the killer to be executed. I told her, "You don't want that. You'll be reminded of his crime every time his case comes up. If he gets life without parole, you'll never hear about him again. You will be able to start to heal."

I don't know if we're bloodthirsty as a society (though the zeal for executions in Texas suggests that we are), but I have seen many families before and after an execution, and I don't think it changes anything. True, the person who died will not commit another offense. But in the gas chamber, in the electric chair, on the injection gurney, or before the firing squad, anger crosses into vengeance. Justice is supposed to be dispassionate. People have a right to express their rage and anger, but I counsel them to make sure that's what they really want. The question I ask them: *When you get what you want, what will you have?*

I challenged inmates: What do you want from your life? What do you want from your relationship with God? Is either goal served by holding onto guilt? Self-inflicted suffering only perpetuates itself and has no other purpose. If you can let it go, I told them, remember that you are worthy, and be open to forgiveness from yourself and God, then you'll find that you are more than ready to live a righteous life.

13

Project IMPACT

In the early 1990s, the Christian men's organization Promise Keepers introduced a program about male accountability that encouraged men to take a leading role in their homes. After receiving some books and other material from Promise Keepers, I asked five San Quentin inmates—Eddie Ramirez, Pat Peralo, Sterling Scott, Kevin Kemp, and a guy named Tim—if they would be interested in participating in an accountability group at San Quentin. I also started seven other groups within the Protestant chapel, but this one was different. These men were from different religious backgrounds—Catholic, Protestant, and Muslim—and various ethnic backgrounds as well. However, each of the men had something very important in common: a strong commitment to live a life of integrity in the correctional setting.

As we started the group, the inmates learned that, in spite of their different religious denominations and family backgrounds, they had much more in common than being behind bars. They were husbands, fathers, brothers, sons, and leaders within their respective religious bodies at the prison. They were men who had made a commitment to go beyond the norm of just doing time; when these men arrived at San Quentin, they decided they would not allow their incarceration to detain them spiritually and emotionally.

After meeting with them for over a year and practicing the principles of accountability, the five guys and I decided that rather than each one receiving a Promise Keepers book, we would have three books shared between six individuals. It was a simple test: would each individual be accountable to read his section of the book, and then give it to his partner in time for him to read it before we met the next Monday? I knew it would require the men to openly communicate with each other, which rarely happens inside the prison walls between men of different faiths and ethnicities.

The response from the inmate population was quite interesting, to say the least. One faith group criticized one of my group members for spending so much time with the Protestant chaplain, but my group members managed to get along and completed their tasks while sharing the books.

It didn't take us long to realize that we were onto something.

AIR and IMPACT Are Developed

It became clear that so many men locked in the dimly lit cells of San Quentin wanted to change the ways that had gotten them there, but it was the most difficult thing in the world for them to admit. Often these men had led bitter, violent lives, in which showing vulnerability was tantamount to pulling the trigger of a gun pointed at their heads. Even after being locked up for many years, they could not admit that they were in pain.

It wasn't just that old habits die hard; it was also the fact that a maximum-security prison can be as fraught with danger as the meanest street. It was safer and easier to fall back on rage, bluster, denial, and show of force—to be the impregnable, I-don't-have-any-problems alpha male. The trouble is that it's a lie.

In my prison ministry, I developed a system to help these tough, hardscrabble men move slowly from stubborn, defensive self-punishment along the road to looking at themselves, accepting their flaws, and discovering their virtues, and most important, humbling themselves before the will of God.

The foundation of the program took the form of an acronym, AIR, which stood for Accountability, Integrity, and Responsibility. This system became the spiritual air in the lungs of some men who were desperate for redemption through Jesus Christ, but did not know how to express their need. Using this system, I was able to break through the shell of intimidation and denial and help a lot of men to forgive themselves and others, to ask God for forgiveness, and to discover the ability to choose the right path in the future.

As we sat around my office one day talking about the program, one of the guys suggested the name IMPACT. I've mentioned that the acronym represents Incarcerated Men Putting Away Childish Things, which is based on 1 Corinthians 13:11: "When I became a man, I put away childish things." And so this accountability and rehabilitation movement was born.

What Inmates Need

At the time I was working with my first Project IMPACT group, Pete Wilson was the governor of California. Part of Wilson's campaign platform was getting tough on crime, and he had repeatedly said that anyone who took a life should do life. Four of the five men in my group were inmates sentenced to life terms, with the possibility of parole. As I watched these men go to the parole board and get denied time and time again, I felt a genuine pain for them. They had clean prison records, had turned their lives around. They'd done everything mandated by the criminal justice system to return to their families and communities. Yet, the parole board repeatedly refused them freedom.

I experienced the pain and frustration of their families as I gave the men opportunities to call home and tell their loved ones the sad news. In some cases, the men didn't want to contact their families and hear their pain. They asked me to call instead.

It became clear that vital principles were lacking in the inmate population that would prevent ex-cons from thriving in the outside world when they were released. As I prayed about the men, it became clear that, until they could see themselves outside the walls of San Quentin Prison, they would not be prepared for release back to their families. I asked them some questions: "Where will you be when you get where you're going? Where do you see yourself once you are released? What do you see yourself doing?"

About two months later, Pat came to the group and said he had something he wanted to share: "It's about that question you asked, Chap. Well, I see myself with my family at the flea market, and we're walking around holding hands. We're just looking, laughing, and talking." About six weeks later, as we were in the middle of our check-in before a meeting started, Kevin told the group he saw himself holding his daughter, hugging her, and letting her know that he loved her. A month later, Sterling told us that he saw himself at home with his dad, playing dominoes and laughing with him. "I'm enjoying being with my dad and my family again," he said. Sometime later, Eddie told the group that he envisioned himself at a big party with his relatives. "Everyone is there, and my family is together again," he said.

I was emboldened to know that my guys still had hope and dreams, even as the parole board was keeping them incarcerated. We had to figure out, via Project IMPACT, how to give feet to those dreams.

A Hard Sell

Let's get an obvious question out of the way: How do you sell accountability to someone who probably won't see any immediate benefit from it? Imagine that you're a prison inmate doing twenty years for armed robbery and assault. Even if you make yourself accountable to yourself, others, and God, you're not getting out. Man's justice is not the same as God's. You can ask God for forgiveness and voila! Instantly, you're saved. But in man's justice system, if you do the crime, you do the time. So, if you're a prisoner with eight years to go before you're even eligible for parole, why care about being accountable?

My answer is that there's a big difference between *detainment* and *incarceration*. Detainment is the holding of your physical body in a cell or other secure area. You're not free to move around as you please. When it's over, you are free. The line is very clear. But incarceration is imprisonment of your mind and spirit. You can be incarcerated anywhere. You don't have to be detained in a jail cell. That means plenty of people who have been freed from detention are still incarcerated, because they are holding onto the same pain, rage, addiction, and rejection of God that landed them in prison in the first place.

It also means that there are people in prison who, while they are detained, are not incarcerated. Because they have become accountable to themselves and to God, forgiven themselves for poor choices, and made themselves instruments of God's will, their bodies may be under lock and key but their spirits are free. These are the people who are most likely to make the internal changes that will result in their being set free from detainment one day. They are the ones with a sense of peace and purpose that you can see, who turn away from their old lives of drugs and crime because they realize (perhaps for the first time) that God really does want something more for them—that they are worthy of so much more.

A Better Goal

It's true that guys in prison do time. San Quentin was built as a place of punishment and it was designed to break spirits and inflict hardship. Initially, the policy of the California Department of Corrections was punishment, not rehabilitation. But, while I was at the prison, the state's policy changed and the administrators came to see that punishment accomplished nothing but imposing meaningless retribution on men who would get out and reoffend. "Vengeance is mine, sayeth the Lord," but God knows that men who are incarcerated in mind and spirit are incapable of doing anything but walking the same path that landed them in prison in the first place. Finally, California arrived at the same conclusion and changed its policy to rehabilitation.

Rehabilitation means to change yourself back into your former self. That meaning can be confusing; if you've been committing crimes as long as you can remember, what can you really change back to? The trick is not to look at your actual past, but the person you could have been if you had chosen to go down a different path. You cannot go back and erase what's already occurred, but you can become the person—in body, mind, and spirit—who would have walked the wise, righteous path back in the day and walk it from this day forward!

The term I use in ministry is *regeneration*, which means to be spiritually restored. Both terms, *rehabilitation* and *regeneration*, speak of change, both seek a positive result. True rehabilitation sends you out into the world with the insight, courage, and faith to walk God's path as it has always been laid out for you. Regeneration sets the standard for kingdom choices. And regeneration will create productive citizens once they are released from prison.

True Freedom

Here's where we see the difference between *accountability* and *responsibility*. Accountability is about an accounting for the past, so you are looking back to what you have already done. When you break with your past and make new choices, you can still own it but you are no longer burdened by it. That's what I mean when I say that you can be detained in prison but no longer incarcerated.

It's moving to see how God's love can transform the heart of even the hardest convict when he lets go of the pain from his past choices. The wisdom of the pain remains, teaching him as he goes forward, but he's no longer chained by that past.

Albert Featherstone, an inmate who was constantly in and out of prison, seemed destined to spend the rest of his life incarcerated either on a life sentence or via the installment plan (a few years in jail, get out, catch a new case, a few more years). After his last arrest, he thought back on what was most meaningful in his life, and he realized that it was the Word of God. While awaiting sentencing, Albert made a decision that he would release the burdens— anger and hopelessness—that had bound him and had kept him in prison for over twenty years.

Albert arrived at San Quentin intent on being an example of the power of God to transform lives. He became the chapel leader in a housing unit and he lived the Word daily. Upon his release, he immediately joined his uncle's church, becoming his uncle's assistant and a youth pastor. Albert went back to school and received his AA, BA, and master's. Today he is a licensed counselor and pastor.

Once he released the anchor that was holding him, Albert was able to soar to new heights.

To be free, we taught the inmates, you have to be removed from your place of incarceration. That means getting rid of people, substances, and other temptations that can steer you back onto your old path. Those things can keep you from allowing God into your daily life—if you're serious about your relationship with God, the one thing you don't want to do is deny His presence in your daily life. Anyone can begin to walk the harder but upward path toward God's will.

What IMPACT Taught

Project IMPACT was conceived and written by incarcerated men as a self-help program for other inmates. The first course we wrote dealt with man's essential makeup, which explained the definition of a son, a man, a husband, and a father. We called it the Male Role Belief System (MRBS). We then taught about image versus reality: the difference between a man and a male, between a husband and a spouse, between a father and a dad. These courses helped inmates to do an inventory and see where they were mentally, emotionally, physically, and spiritually, so that they could make corrections in their perceptions and behavior.

The last part of the course was "How Do You Measure Up?" Each session of the workbook was designed to move the inmates toward a level of accountability. Then we addressed the idea that they first have to be responsible to themselves, living lives of value and purpose. Then we worked on how they could be responsible to their families: avoiding a behavior that may delay their departure and extend the family's suffering. Sending home money they earned from their jobs, even if it was only enough to cover the bridge toll and something from the vending machines. Not calling home collect often to save their families some money.

Finally, we used the session to discuss how they could make the time they were doing help their communities, by sharing their stories with youth groups and meeting with representatives to discuss the community's needs. They could establish a level of community accountability for when they were released. We used AIR and a three-tiered philosophy of working on self, then helping one's family, and finally making amends and working on bettering the community.

As a part of the course we decided to have a holiday party for the children. Many times, when the kids came into the visiting room, they did not get the attention they deserved. Visits were short, and the inmates and their family members tried to get as much discussed and worked out as possible.

For the party, money was generated and, with the assistance of our chapel volunteers, a large number of gifts were purchased. Each inmate wrote down what he thought his child would want. We brought the gifts into the chapel and, after prayer, the men wrapped them. I remember a guy named Big D had tears in his eyes as he prepared gifts for his kids. Some guys admitted that they had never wrapped a gift before. All the gifts were placed in bags with the children's names on them.

On the evening of the party, after the food and songs, the men went to the Christmas tree we had decorated and started to call their children up to get their gifts. There were a lot of tears from the men, as well as from the adult family members. One memory we still laugh about is how one little boy fell asleep on his rocking horse. He rode it so long it rocked him to sleep right next to the tree.

Rhinos, Elephants, and IMPACT

In 1999, the TV news show *60 Minutes* broadcast a report about juvenile delinquency. Bob Simon, a reporter, documented a gang of unruly teenagers who'd gone on a wild killing spree. But the show wasn't about your typical juvenile delinquents—it was about young elephants in Africa. I didn't see the show when it originally aired, but Pat saw it and was very excited when he came to the Project IMPACT meeting the next day.

"That's it," Pat said. "That's the answer! That's what's wrong in our communities!"

We asked Pat to explain what he saw. We shared the story with one of our volunteers, Collette Carroll, who was able to persuade someone at CBS to send us a videotape of the show. We watched it together a couple of weeks later. It was about a group of young male elephants that were killing white rhinoceroses at South Africa's Pilanesberg Park. Game rangers had spent many years protecting the white rhinos, who were on the verge of extinction, but a pack of juvenile male elephants had killed thirty-nine rhinos, about 10 percent of the park's population. The juvenile elephants also were acting aggressively toward tourist vehicles. Game rangers had to shoot five of the elephants because they were so unruly.[1]

After studying the young male elephants for several months, zoologists finally figured out that they were unmanageable because they'd grown up without role models. About twenty years earlier, the young elephants had been taken from South Africa's largest conservation area, Kruger National Park, because the elephant population was too large. Game rangers killed their parents because they were too big to move and transported the young elephants to Pilanesberg Park. Before too long, the park had an entire generation of traumatized orphan elephants, which were thrown together without any adults to teach them how to behave. They were left to wander aimlessly and figure out life on their own.

At the end of the segment, zoologists introduced older bull elephants to Pilanesberg Park. I'm sure you can guess what happened next: The young elephants stopped killing the rhinos. The scientists said the bigger, older elephants established a new hierarchy, in part by sparring with the younger elephants over mating partners. The younger elephants weren't as sexually active, so they had less testosterone. I believe there was probably a conversation between the juveniles and the adult males, which probably went something like this, "We're elephants. We don't kill rhinos." After the bull elephants arrived, not one rhino was killed.[2]

IMPACT Spreads

The *60 Minutes* segment ended up being a turning point for Project IMPACT. It was our gateway into working with youth and expanding our program into communities outside the prison. The guys recognized that a large number of children of incarcerated men end up becoming criminals themselves. It becomes a tragic cycle, in which children are left without a father or mother at home and turn to crime, drugs, gangs, and violence to fill the void. I can't tell you how many of the inmates I worked with had a parent or sibling who also was incarcerated.

For nearly two decades, Project IMPACT has served the inmates of San Quentin, helping them break down rationalization, denial, and displacement issues they used to avoid accepting responsibility for their crimes. In 2005, the California Department of Corrections and Rehabilitation chose Project IMPACT to pilot at three youth correctional facilities to help curb violence and gang activity among youth offenders. An evaluation of the program revealed that youth offenders who graduated from Project IMPACT were less likely to commit violent acts while they were incarcerated and after they were released.[3]

With my help and the assistance of volunteers, our group wrote a curriculum that addresses aggressive behavior among men and women and boys and girls. Man's Essential Makeup and Woman's Essential Makeup are the foundational courses. The men learn about relationships, addictions, violence prevention, ethics, financial literacy, and a probation life plan. For women, the courses include identity theft, the cycle of abuse, relationships, ethics, and financial literacy.

The program's facilitators are paroled male and female ex-offenders (post-crime achievers), who are the most effective at having an impact on young men and women through self-testimony. What better way to steer a young person on the right track than to have him or her listen to adults who paid the price for the same mistakes the youths are making?

The Project IMPACT program involves twelve weekly two-hour sessions in which youths meet with large groups of thirty inmates. We discuss the topic of the day for about twenty to thirty minutes, and then the class breaks up into smaller groups of about ten to fourteen youths. In the smaller groups, the topic is thoroughly discussed for more than an hour.

There are also lessons on violence prevention, substance abuse and other addictions, relationships, ethics, financial literacy, gang lifestyles, and parole and probation planning. The lessons are designed to assist youths by enabling them to redefine who they are and to assess the meaning and direction of their future lives. More than anything else, we try to convince these kids that their lives aren't over because of their past mistakes, and that they can still lead healthy and productive lives if they start to make the right choices.

We all face times when we walk along that narrow ledge between a life of hard-won peace and joy and a life of enticing, short-term pleasure. It is not easy to choose the righteous path, especially when the unrighteous path appears simpler, more satisfying, and more socially acceptable. But those who make the hard choice and walk the straight and narrow find the wonder of God's grace.

We can choose righteousness, gratitude, giving, and spiritual well-being, or we can choose quick gratification that ends up in despair, illegal activity, pain, and loss. At those moments, we stand poised between riches and ruins; only with an understanding of faith and important principles in life can we be assured of choosing the right path.

We also launched a similar program for women: WISE (Women Incarcerated Still Enduring). Then in 1999, my wife, Angel, and I along with Danny Rifkin, the past manager of the Grateful Dead, designed the concept for Project AVARY (Alternative Ventures for At Risk Youth), which gives the children of inmates an opportunity to leave their communities and connect with other children facing similar challenges. Danny took the idea and has made Project AVARY a national model.

Dreams Come True

As Project IMPACT started to make a real difference at San Quentin, an amazing thing started to take place. Pat, who was the first member of our original Project IMPACT group to say that he could see himself outside the prison walls, was finally declared suitable for parole and the governor granted his release. One Saturday, Pat called me because he wanted me to know that he was at the flea market with his family, just as he'd envisioned. More than a year after Pat went home, Kevin was recommended for parole. The governor also approved Kevin's release, and he even cited Project IMPACT as one of the reasons for his approval, because he believed the program could make a difference on the outside. Shortly after Kevin went home, he requested permission to see his terminally ill daughter in Oregon. It was unheard of for life-term parolees to be allowed to travel outside of a fifty-mile radius, much less out of state. Yet, that is the vision Kevin saw upon his release. She was sick the entire time Kevin was in prison, and he was able to visit with her and hold her shortly before she died.

After Kevin was released from San Quentin, Sterling went to the parole board and was found suitable for release. After Sterling went home, I called him and he was playing dominoes with his Pops. Eddie was the last member of our original Project IMPACT group who was granted parole. Because Eddie was sentenced for a crime he committed in Southern California, he had to move back there to serve his parole. On the weekend of Eddie's release, I spoke with him on the phone, and there was a lot of noise in the background. He was at a relative's home for a family reunion.

Oddly enough, each man was released in the order in which he reported seeing himself outside the walls of San Quentin during our meetings. Without these men seeing themselves free, I don't think Project IMPACT would have been anything more than a deferred dream. Today, the men are loving husbands, caring fathers, attentive sons, and are recognized by their religious communities as men who are accountable and live lives of integrity.

Each of them still works as a senior facilitator at Project IMPACT and has profound effects on his community's youth. Patrick is working as a union plumber in San Jose, California. Eddie is married and lives in Sunnyvale, California. Kevin is a gospel recording artist, works as a minister of music at a church, and is a motivational speaker to youth organizations, churches, schools, and community groups. Sterling wrote and self-published a 602-page memoir, *The Weeds of Society*. He conducted a law seminar at Stanford University Law School and has worked as a consultant for a prestigious San Francisco law firm. Kevin might have been speaking for all of them when he said his mission in life is to keep "boys in the hood from becoming men in the pen." I couldn't be prouder of them.

Leonard Neal was not a member of the original group, yet soon after IMPACT was started in the prison, he was voted in as a facilitator. I mention Leonard because of all the families I worked with while at San Quentin, the Neal family represented the best model of consistency and dependability. Leonard's wife, Eleanor, visited the prison each week and made sure that Leonard was actively involved in the lives of his three children. Leonard did twenty-four years, eleven months, and seven days. During that time, his two oldest children graduated from high school. Those children have gone on to graduate from college and are high school teachers. Leonard exemplified the principles of Accountability, Integrity, and Responsibility. Leonard is the chief operating officer of the organization.

In all my years in prison, I ministered to only a handful of guys who didn't want to be forgiven, to relieve their agony, and to find some sort of peace, even if they were serving life sentences. I think that's true of all of us: We're all serving a life sentence in God's world, and if we choose to, we can turn it into a prison all by ourselves. But we can also choose to change who we are and how we live in this world, and the miracle from God is that with a single choice—the decision to give ourselves over to the Lord and obey His will—we can go from incarceration to freedom in an instant.

14

Faith by Numbers

D<small>URING MY TIME AT</small> S<small>AN</small> Quentin, I tried many new ideas to bring God's grace and mercy to as many men as possible. Sometimes I succeeded; other times, I wasn't so lucky. In the end, I was only the messenger.

In 1990, I thought far outside the box (the chapel) again. After consulting with Bishop Frank Costantino, Chaplain Ray Hoekstra, and convict-turned-minister Jack "Murph the Surf" Murphy, I helped organize a reunion of Living Epistles—former inmates who came together from across the country to represent the power of Christ to save and change lives. This San Quentin Homecoming was the first reunion of its kind in the country and has become a national model for making use of the talents of post-crime achievers. I brought in pro athletes like Football Hall of Fame quarterback Steve Young and Baseball Hall of Fame catcher Gary Carter to help minister to the inmates. I knew that their fame would give them a lot of credibility with the guys. I broke the unspoken prison culture rules (such as "inmates from different races don't mix"), and, I think, changed some lives.

From Inmates to Athletes

For nearly a quarter century, I've also ministered to many of the world's most famous and highest-paid athletes. I worked as a team chaplain for the NBA's Golden State Warriors, NFL's San Francisco 49ers, and Major League Baseball's San Francisco Giants. My venture into working with professional athletes started with a random phone call in 1990.

"Hello, Mr. Smith? This is Jim Fitzgerald, owner of the NBA's Golden State Warriors. We were wondering if you'd like to come do our chapel services before our games."

"Who is this playing a joke on me?" I asked the guy. "You know I don't like basketball."

"Reverend Smith, this really is Jim Fitzgerald, and I really do own the Warriors," he said. "We were given your name as someone we might want to talk to about conducting our chapels. Will you at least come to the team's Christmas party and give an opening prayer?"

Obviously, I was embarrassed about telling him I didn't like basketball, but I'd always preferred baseball and football. I took my wife, Angel, to the Christmas party, and the owners handed her a gold watch as a gift. "You better take this job," she told me. Basketball was always Angel's favorite sport; the watch was an added bonus.

The Golden State Warriors bought off my wife, and I went to work with them at the end of the 1990-91 season. I've worked for the franchise for twenty-four seasons, through all of its ups and downs. Angel and I treated going to the games as sort of a date night. We would ride from our house on the prison grounds to Oakland and talk about our day and sometimes leave early and go out for soul food.

Replacement

In 1997, Pat Richie, who was the 49ers chaplain, wanted to take a sabbatical, and asked if I'd take over his duties on a temporary basis. Pat had previously invited me to conduct chapel before 49ers games. On December 3, 1990, I delivered the pregame chapel service for the New York Giants before they played the 49ers on *Monday Night Football*. I took my father to the game. He refused to remove his 49ers cap and jacket, which I thought he needed to do to show the Giants we were neutral. "Son, if this is going keep them from winning, they don't deserve to win," he said. "I'm not taking this stuff off." The 49ers won the game, 7–3.

Pat had a dream of the teams praying together. He conceived of the postgame prayer huddle so fans could see the contrast between the all-too-familiar images of the out-of-control athlete and the guys who show there is more substance to their lives than just football. I was blessed to play a small part in what is now as much a part of the game as the kickoff.

I told Pat that I'd be happy to fill in for him for a season, but only if he would let me work with the Giants as well. Being a big baseball fan, I loved going to the games and taking my kids with me. I conducted the chapel services before Giants home games every Sunday.

Pat was gone for a full season and, when he came back, he decided he didn't want to be a team chaplain anymore. Steve Mariucci, who coached the 49ers from 1997 to 2002, called me into his office and offered me the chaplain position.

"You're a blue-chipper," Mariucci told me. "I want you on my team." Mariucci had been a college coach and there, the best recruits were called "blue-chippers." I felt very emotional to hear him say that. I was excited about the opportunity to develop the ministry. I was a placeholder for Pat and did not want to change anything he had done, since I believed he was coming back. As it turned out, the best ministry plan for athletes was the one Pat put in place.

Different Audiences, Messages

You might think it was difficult to transform my ministry from serving down-on-their-luck inmates, some of whom would never set foot outside the prison walls again, to serving some of the world's biggest celebrities. In many ways, though, working with pro athletes wasn't much different from ministering to incarcerated men. As I ministered to inmates, I tried to persuade them that things weren't as bad as they seemed, and that it was important to live a life of integrity, even if it was behind bars. Conversely, professional athletes might believe they're on top of the world. I had to convince the pro athletes that things weren't as good as they might seem, and that there were still plenty of potential pitfalls in their lives, despite their newly found fortune and fame.

It's hard to convince some pro athletes that they're not bullet-proof. Pro sports are some of the country's highest-paid professions, millions of fans watch the athletes at games and on television, and they're paid handsomely to endorse products. Americans put pro athletes and movie stars on pedestals. It might seem that pro athletes don't have a need for anything. But many pro athletes I work with face the same problems that you and I do. Many of them grew up in poverty, then were suddenly handed riches to play a game. Some athletes are financially illiterate because they've never had much money before, and family members and friends might be ready to pounce on their instant fortune. Pro athletes face myriad temptations on the road, such as extramarital sex, drugs, and alcohol, and it is part of my job to challenge them to make the right choices. I try to explain to them that every decision they make should please God.

I believe that the team chaplain's role is to remind people that there has to be a balance to life. My job was to talk athletes through slumps and droughts but, more important, to minister to them about their faith, families, triumphs, and struggles. I cannot force a person to convert to Christianity. But every athlete I've ever worked with knew I wasn't going to judge him and was still going to be available for anything he might need—even if he never attended one of my chapel services. I can only share with these men what God has done in my life and continue to show them love, compassion, and sincerity. I can't change a person's heart—that is God's job.

Sometimes, I use my experiences at San Quentin to relay a lesson to pro athletes. While I was conducting a chapel service before the Giants played the Cincinnati Reds one Sunday, I shared the story of Michael Todd, one of the inmates. Michael had been a great football player in high school but was sent to prison a couple of times for drug offenses. Michael was a skilled player on our eight-man tackle football team. He'd earned the moniker Slate Rock many years earlier because he was so strong. At the time, we were playing teams from the military bases and, after a few seasons, they refused to play us because Michael was running all over them. We went undefeated two years in a row.

After I shared the story of Slate Rock with the major leaguers, Reds outfielder Greg Vaughn, who was sitting next to Deion Sanders, spoke up. I noticed Greg had tears in his eyes when he said, "His name isn't Slate Rock. It's Michael Todd. He was my running back in high school. I was his blocking back, and he was the best there ever was." Michael and Greg had attended John F. Kennedy High School together in Sacramento. Because they chose divergent paths in life, their lives ended up turning out much differently. When I was finished with the tale, Deion said, "Pastor, that's the best story I've ever heard!"

T-Train: Tragedy

During my career as a team chaplain, I witnessed a handful of sport's greatest achievements, many great wins, and a few heartbreaking losses, along with some of the most devastating tragedies for men who were thought to be invincible. One of the saddest days of my long tenure as a team chaplain occurred on August 20, 2005. The 49ers were playing an exhibition game against the Denver Broncos on the road. Thomas "T-Train" Herrion, a twenty-three-year-old reserve guard, was one of the most popular players on the team. Thomas grew up in a drug-infested neighborhood in Fort Worth, Texas, but was determined to lead a better life. He attended a junior college before transferring to the University of Utah, where he played for Coach Urban Meyer. Thomas played one season in NFL Europe and the next season with the Dallas Cowboys before joining the 49ers in 2004.

Thomas wasn't even sure he was going to make the 49ers squad, but the guys absolutely loved having him in the locker room. He had a really jovial personality, and loved to sing and play the piano. Near the end of the exhibition game on a cool night in Denver, Thomas played about twenty plays on offense. He shook hands with a few Denver players afterward, interacted with fans, and joked with the team's nutritionist. In the locker room, the team gathered around Coach Mike Nolan and recited the Lord's Prayer. As soon as we said, "Amen," Thomas collapsed. He was rushed to a hospital where he died. His cause of death was determined to be heart disease. His father, a pastor, had died of a stroke.

After Thomas passed away, the 49ers let me get the team together, and I ministered to them. Five days later, I flew to Dallas with more than a dozen players, coaches, and other administrators for Thomas's funeral. Meyer spoke during the service, and Eric Heitmann, one of his fellow offensive linemen, wrote a piano piece that he played during the funeral. Otis Amey, one of our wide receivers, sang.

What the 49ers did next was amazing: team owners Denise and

John York bought Herrion's mother a new home, and the players paid to furnish it. Thomas's dream had been to play in the NFL long enough to buy his mother a new house. He wasn't a superstar or really significant player, but to the team he seemed as if he was the most important person in the world.

Even today, the 49ers still have T-Train's locker in place, with a small photo of him on a shelf and his shoes and other personal effects still there. The 49ers established the Thomas Herrion Memorial Award in 2005, which is given to the rookie or first-year player who best exemplifies Thomas's dream. The award goes to a player who has taken advantage of every opportunity, turned it into a positive situation, and made his dream a reality.

Obstacles Are for Everyone

I've learned that it doesn't matter if a player is a superstar or bench warmer—chances are he is going to face obstacles, on and off the field, during his career. 49ers star Vernon Davis is one of the highest-paid tight ends in NFL history; he signed a five-year, $37 million contract extension with the team in 2010. But it took a lot of soul searching for Vernon to get to where he is today.

In 2008, Vernon was on the verge of self-destruction, spending a great deal of time in extracurricular activities. Mike Singletary, who was the team's coach at the time, banished Vernon to the locker room with ten minutes left in a game against the Seattle Seahawks on October 27, 2008. Vernon wasn't sure why he'd been sent off the field. When he saw Mike after the game, Mike told him that as soon as he put the team ahead of himself, everything would happen for him. At the time, Vernon was consumed with his stats—his individual victories rather than the team's.

Mike's words of advice were prophetic, but Vernon had to overcome his fears of abandonment and failure to become the player that everyone believed he could be. Vernon beat his issues when he made Christ first in his life. His parents were both drug addicts, and his grandmother, Adeline Davis, raised him and his six siblings in Washington, D.C. Vernon was an All-American at the University of Maryland, and his brother Vontae was a standout cornerback at Illinois who also plays in the NFL. On Tuesday, December 29, 2009, the day Vernon learned that he had been voted to his first Pro Bowl, I baptized him in the presence of his family.

After Vernon began to reach his potential in the NFL, an unthinkable tragedy struck his family. His younger brother Michael, who had battled mental illness for much of his life, was charged in May 2012 with murdering a man who was visiting Washington, D.C. According to police, Michael beat the man with a claw hammer. He also was charged for a handful of other attacks in the neighborhood. Michael was later put in a medical facility and found unsuitable to stand trial. Vernon was stunned by the events and returned home to care for his grandmother.

Another player had a different problem. On November 10, 2012, I was at the 49ers' team hotel. We had just finished chapel and I noticed our second-year quarterback, Colin Kaepernick, was looking a bit down. I sat next to him and asked him to tell me what was going on. Colin wanted to be more involved in the game. Colin was used to being the playmaker, as he was in high school and college. We talked about his college career, how he started behind another player, then replaced him when he was hurt and kept the job. I told Colin just to be faithful and to continue to have a positive attitude and he would be used at the right moment. The next day, during the first half of a game against the St. Louis Rams, starting quarterback Alex Smith was injured and Colin was put into the game. While the game was going on, I texted him: "Wow." Colin kept the starting job and led the 49ers to Super Bowl XLVII at the end of the 2012 season.

The Toughest Cases

While ministering to athletes after tragedies is perhaps my most difficult work with the pro teams, helping players come to grips with the end of their playing careers can also be traumatic. I was with Steve Young on the night his career ended at Arizona on September 27, 1999. As the 49ers' quarterback, Steve was a two-time NFL Most Valuable Player, MVP of Super Bowl XXIX, and he threw for more than thirty-three thousand yards with 232 touchdowns. But Steve suffered at least seven concussions during his career, and he knew after his last concussion in a game against the Cardinals that his career was over. 49ers running back Lawrence Phillips missed a block on the play, and Cardinals safety Aeneas Williams inadvertently kneed Steve in the back of the head. When Steve was taken out of the game, I walked off the field with him and carried his helmet.

While Steve was undergoing concussion exams in the locker room, he became belligerent with the team doctors, shouting, "I have to get back on the field! If I don't get back on the field, I'll never play again." However, the doctors had concluded that he had suffered too many concussions and should not play football any longer. Steve's quitting was a medical decision. He missed the final thirteen games of the 1999 season and retired the next summer.

Steve and his wife, Barbara, were involved in my ministry at San Quentin. One time, while Steve, Barb, former 49ers offensive linemen Jesse Sapolu and Steve Wallace, tight end Greg Clark, and others were in the prison, an alarm sounded because someone had been stabbed in the forehead. There were guards running everywhere, and Steve panicked and took off running! His wife was standing next to me against a wall. We both laughed.

Watching Steve's career end so suddenly was difficult, but I witnessed at least one medical miracle while working with the 49ers. In January 1999, running back Garrison Hearst broke the fibula bone in his left leg on the first play from scrimmage in a playoff game against the Atlanta Falcons. Garrison had just signed a five-year contract worth $15.1 million and was considered the team's future. Doctors initially feared they might have to amputate his leg, due to the severity of his injury. Blood vessels and nerves were damaged, and doctors worried he might suffer necrosis, in which the tissue and bone in his leg would die.

The night before Garrison's surgery, his grandmother went to his hospital room and wrapped a rag around his injured leg. She prayed and rubbed oil on it. Garrison told me his ankle started burning. In July 1999, an orthopedist performed a second surgery to try to stimulate blood flow to his foot. The surgeon told him, "Young man, I prayed about it last night, and God told me you're already healed. We're going to do this surgery, but you're going to be fine."

After a two-year absence, Garrison returned to the field in

2001 and ran for 1,206 yards with four touchdowns. Garrison was the Associated Press 2001 Comeback Player of the Year. He played in parts of three more NFL seasons before retiring in 2004. After nearly having his leg amputated, Garrison fought back and had a great NFL career.

I try to minister to the inmates and offer them advice to the best of my ability, but I have to admit that my best intentions sometimes don't work out. The day before the 49ers played the Dallas Cowboys on September 24, 2000, I was riding on the team bus to go to a walk-through at Texas Stadium. During the ride, I made the mistake of telling wide receivers Terrell Owens, J. J. Stokes, and receivers coach George Stewart how people loved the Cowboys. "I used to live here," I said. "They love this team."

"Man, they couldn't even finish their dome stadium," Terrell said. "There's a hole in the middle of the roof!" We laughed.

"No, man, there's a star in the middle of the field," I said. "You're supposed to stand on the star and look up at God. This is God's team. He'll see you."

Well, Terrell scored two touchdowns in the 49ers' 41–24 victory over the Cowboys the next day. I'm sure you can guess what he did after he scored: He ran to the star in the middle of the field, extended his arms, and looked up at the hole in the roof. After Terrell did it a second time, Cowboys safety George Teague leveled him, starting a fracas between the teams.

I'm sorry to say my attempt at humor cost Terrell a one-game suspension and a week's pay in fines. We were still able to laugh about the incident, though, and Terrell even gave me a game touchdown ball. I can honestly say that he was only joking, and wasn't trying to disrespect the Cowboys.

End of an Era

I'm still continuing my ministry with the 49ers and Warriors; I stopped working with the Giants in 2005. In August 2006, I retired as chaplain at San Quentin Prison. It wasn't an easy decision, but the death of one of the inmates had a profound impact on me.

The inmate's name was Tank Parrish. He'd been in juvenile halls and prisons since he was twelve years old. Tank came to the chapel one day and said he wanted to sing. My guys didn't want him to be a part of the choir because he smelled. He didn't know anything about hygiene and had a foul odor about him. I told the guys that if they did not find a way to include Tank in the choir, I would shut it down. They didn't think I was serious, but I did it.

To me, Tank represented Matthew 25:40: "And the King will answer and say to them, 'Assuredly, I say to you, inasmuch as you did it to one of the least of these My brethren, you did it to Me.'" The guys finally agreed to let Tank participate, and once he started singing (from the back row away from the microphone), his life changed for the better. He started showering, shaving, and wearing clean clothes to chapel service on Sunday. Tank finally had something to look forward to and a reason to live.

However, in October 2004, he was on his way to the bathroom near the chapel, and I heard him scream, "Chap, help! Chap, help!" He was leaning against the bathroom door and fell into my arms when I got to him. "Chap, don't leave me," Tank told me.

I shouted, "Man down!" Chaplain Hassan blew his whistle for help. When correctional officers arrived, one of them looked at Tank and said, "Oh, that's just Parrish. He took some bad dope."

They'd called for a wheelchair, which was being pushed across the yard. An ambulance was finally called, and Tank was transported to the prison hospital. Tank had suffered an aneurysm. He spent two days on life support at an outside hospital before he died in my arms.

A few days after Tank died, I took a sabbatical. I found that I couldn't keep operating on autopilot anymore, as I'd done after the executions. It was different. It's crazy, but I realized that to many people, someone like Tank, a little guy who sometimes smelled bad, was just a number and truly did not matter. His family lived across the bridge from the prison and never visited him. Some of the guys thought he was insignificant, and the medical staff simply thought he took some bad dope. For Tank, the so-called bad dope was the first crime he committed as a young child. He became addicted to a life of crime.

Tank's death was a deep wound for me, one that caused me to pause and reflect on my future at San Quentin Prison. Many guys in the prison were much worse than Tank. He was not much of anything to the people who didn't know him, yet I had witnessed his transformation and the joy he felt in serving God.

I often wonder, *how could God allow Tank to die in my arms?* I'll never forget his eyes searching for help and hearing him say, "Chap, don't leave me." That hurt me immensely. His death was a tragedy that took the joy of working at San Quentin away for me. I could not find it within myself to go into the prison, see the bathroom and hallway where he died, and still have the same sense of satisfaction about working with the inmates.

I'll never forget how the medical technician assistant showed no concern about Tank. I practically had to beg to get an ambulance to transport him. Clearly, there was something wrong. I wondered how I could continue to work in an environment where people didn't care about the value of a man's life. It was then that I realized I was tired and couldn't be the prison chaplain any longer.

While I was away on medical leave after Tank died, I realized that I never had anyone with whom I could share my thoughts about the executions, deaths, and the misery suffered during my time at San Quentin. After each execution or inmate death, and after calling his family to notify them about the inmate's passing, I went back to work. I never allowed myself to process what I was feeling or what I had witnessed. I believe that over a period of time I became indifferent to suffering. Prison can do that to you. I felt that I gave my best to San Quentin, but at the end of my career there, my spirit was broken, and I had to leave.

Afterword

W<small>HEN</small> I <small>STARTED WORKING AT</small> San Quentin Prison, I didn't have a clue about what was in store for me. When I left after working for twenty-three years as a chaplain, I still had a lot of unanswered questions about the place.

I wondered what I could have done to help inmates like Tank Parrish. I wondered about the value of segregating inmates by race. I wondered what I could have done to save more men and bring them closer to Jesus Christ. I believed that I had spent my time wisely and tried to help as many men as possible, but I suspect I could have done more. The chapel program was fine and was helping a lot of lost souls, but at the end I don't believe I was giving God my best.

Now that I've retired from the prison ministry, a lot of people have asked what it was like working in a place with such a notorious reputation. I have to admit that there were times I was concerned for my safety. I remember one occasion when the prison was in a state of emergency. The inmates were locked in their cells twenty-four hours a day, and they were becoming quite restless. I had to go to the fifth tier of Carson Section to notify an inmate about a death in his family. As I made my way up the stairs, the inmates were screaming at me and throwing whatever garbage they could get their hands on.

As I was leaving the tier after talking with the inmate, another prisoner called for me. His cell was dark and, for some reason, I knew that he was up to something. As I got closer to his cell, I saw only a flash. He had thrown feces and urine on me. There was nothing I could have done to stop it. The other inmates laughed as I left the tier. I went to the chapel and took off my clothes, used a hose to rinse off, then put on my baptism clothes. I bagged the dirty clothes and threw them away. I never told my wife about the incident.

Another time I baptized an inmate who was HIV positive. As I brought him out of the water, he started to spit water in my face and eyes. I was frightened that I had contracted the disease from him. I was so concerned that I was monitored and tested by my doctors for a year. It was during the early stages of HIV/AIDS, when we still didn't know much about how the disease was contracted, and the virus was beginning to make its way into San Quentin. A number of homosexual inmates were experiencing life-changing events and wanted to be baptized like a lot of the other inmates. Yes, I was frightened and so were the members of my inmate leadership team, because of our initial ignorance about the disease.

Prison Has to Exist

Despite the fears I experienced, I have relied upon a saying that has biblical significance: "The Law is for the Lawless." A prison has to exist for certain people. Some are lawless to their core and, even if given an opportunity to change into law-abiding citizens, they would turn down the offer.

Some fathers and sons sleep under the same roof for the first time while in prison. Families have reunions in prison. One time, I received a call from someone in Richmond, California, asking me to inform an inmate that his son had been killed. I wrote the name down and his cell location. A few hours later, I received a call asking me to inform an inmate that his brother had been killed in Richmond. I wrote down the inmate's name and his cell location. As I prepared to get the inmates, I realized they were housed together.

I had them escorted to my office. I informed them of the deaths. The son cried, but his father said, "Come on, man, be a man. He died a soldier." I learned that the father had never slept a single night under the same roof with his son who was killed, and the first time he slept in the same location with his other son was when the youngster was sentenced to prison and sent to San Quentin. It was a real tragedy but, sadly, their story wasn't unique.

For our society, Death Row is the final stop for men and women who have committed the most heinous of crimes. But it was my calling to bring the Word to the least, including the men who would never walk outside of Condemned Row. I met condemned inmates like Lawrence Sigmund Bittaker who, along with Roy Norris, were known as the Toolbox Killers. They kidnapped, raped, tortured, and murdered five teenage girls in Southern California in 1979. To me, Bittaker represented evil. He had no remorse for his crimes and was a whiner and complainer. The man had no regard for life, and I imagine if he were released he would pick up where he left off.

Then there was another condemned inmate who was the son of a Baptist pastor. He went into a store with some guys who robbed it and killed the owner. He did not plan the crime; he only went along for the ride. Once the crime was discovered, his father told him to do the right thing: tell the truth about what happened. The son did as his father told him. In that crime, five guys went into the store. The son did not have a gun, nor did he touch the cash register. The son told the truth, yet he was convicted and sent to Death Row. The other guys went to trial and received sentences of twenty-five years to life. The shooter received a life without parole. In my opinion, the son does not belong on Death Row.

Because I spent so much time ministering to inmates on Death Row, people often ask me if I believe in the death penalty. Although I believe in supporting the laws of our country, I think the death penalty is a flawed concept, because condemned men have later been acquitted of the crimes of which they were accused. I cannot in good conscience support a flawed concept that is so final in application. And as I said earlier, I don't believe the victims' families and friends receive any sense of closure by killing the men and women who harmed their loved ones.

Death, Destruction—and Hope

As you've seen in these pages, prison is also an environment of hope and faith. Men whom society has cast aside due to their crimes must come to realize they are not their crimes, and then decide if it is worth it to move forward with their lives. I met men who had never committed a prior crime—never even been issued a traffic citation—but suddenly snapped, murdered a friend, and were sentenced to life in prison or death. Those men had to decide if it was worthwhile to go on with their lives. They had to find something within themselves to combat the invading forces of evil, which tried to convince them that they were their crimes, that they were murderers, and there wasn't a chance they would ever be anything else. In prison, hope has a conversation with reality, and hope polishes the rough spots of reality with faith, which says, "Therefore if any man be in Christ, he is a new creation, behold old things are passed away, all things become new."

Many inmates are people with hope. They are men and women with families. Inmates are people with problems, and their problems sometimes cause them to live in an environment lacking trust and rational thinking. Some people deserve to be detained in manmade facilities. Some people deserve to be given a second chance. On any given Sunday, we can probably say the same things about many of the people sitting in congregations across this great land.

Looking back on my career, I think God was able to use me to bring people closer to Him. Everyone talked about San Quentin being the "Dungeon of Doom." I don't believe any place is so hopeless that God can't do something there. I wanted to be able to show that, even in a place like San Quentin, people could find something of value. I did my best to help the men realize that there was still a reason for hope.

Reflections

I've been blessed to work with inmates and sports heroes. I have traveled across the United States, visiting many prisons and sports stadiums. I have been to World Series and Super Bowls. I've sat with inmates as they waited to die and once held hands with a player who said "Amen," then died. God has allowed me to experience so much in life. Yet, the greatest joy I have realized was watching my children being born and seeing them develop with all of the trials and tribulations life brought.

From the day I walked through the iron gates of San Quentin Prison, I never regretted being called to the ministry. Each day presented a different challenge. Some days I hated working with the prison staff, and felt they were more toxic than the inmates. Racism was a hazard of the job and it didn't come only from the inmates. A guard who worked the back entrance gate for staff vehicles had the Confederate flag on his license plate. He was proud of his beliefs. We had other staff members who called inmates racially loaded names. Despite the challenges, I never wanted to quit. In fact, I felt I couldn't quit—until Tank died in my arms.

I loved the men and seeing their lives changed. I loved seeing families made whole again. I loved seeing barriers broken and reconciliation and healing take place. Where else in ministry can you see God's transforming power at work in such a significant manner on a daily basis? Each day I went to work, I expected to be part of a miracle. I expected God to do something special.

As I look back on my life and career at San Quentin, it's clear that God's hand was guiding me. I grew from being an angry kid to being a person void of compassion to being someone who heard God speak to him on a hospital gurney. My dad said, "You are a rebel, but you are God's rebel and we're going to make it." And we did.

Acknowledgments

WITH GRATITUDE AND A MEASURE of love, I wish to thank my dear friends who have been so important and encouraging in helping me understand the value of what it means to have a story and to live the story and to share the story. Your support and encouragement during my journey behind the walls was the voice of reason on so many occasions when I was not sure if I should continue or I could continue.

To my guys behind the walls and outside the walls, you allowed me to grow as a man and pastor; with you I learned the meaning of hope. Thank you.

To all of the volunteers who made the San Quentin ministry so special, without your kindness, selflessness, courage, dedication, and agape there would not be a story. The hours you gave to make the lives of the men and their families richer was Matthew 25 lived out on a daily basis.

To the San Francisco 49ers, the Golden State Warriors, and the San Francisco Giants, what an unbelievable level of trust you displayed in allowing me to minister to the players, families, and staff associated with your organizations. Your thoughtfulness and the care shown to my family and me are appreciated. And to each of the players who allowed me see them beyond their jersey number, what joy I have experienced watching you grow and mature.

To the staff of IMPACT and WISE I am so proud of you and what you are accomplishing. Lives are being changed from the inside out and we are "breaking the cycle." Good Job . . . Good Job!

To the men of the greatest fraternity in the world, the men of the Omega Psi Phi Fraternity, Incorporated. To my Brothers from Mu Gamma Chapter, I am so blessed that God allowed us to experience such a special journey at Bishop College.

In closing, I cannot fail to thank Mark Schlabach. Your patience and understanding as this project was unfolding was reassuring. You allowed me to share some insights and pains, which we did not include; yet they were necessary to share to get us to this point. Your sensitivity is appreciated.

Notes

Chapter 2

1. James Montague, "The Third Man: The Forgotten Black Power Hero," CNN, April 25, 2012. http://edition.cnn .com/2012/04/24/sport/olympics-norman-black-power/.

Chapter 5

1. Francesca Levy, "America's 25 Richest Counties," *Forbes*, March 4, 2010. http://www.forbes.com/2010/03/04/america-richest -counties-lifestyle-real-estate-wealthy-suburbs.html.
2. Dan Simon and Scott Thompson, "California Lawmaker Proposes Selling San Quentin Prison," CNN, April 1, 2009. http:// edition.cnn.com/2009/US/03/31/oceanfront.prison/.

Chapter 6

1. Jack Olsen, *Last Man Standing: The Tragedy and Triumph of Geronimo Pratt* (New York: Anchor, 2001), 78.
2. Richard Gonzalez, "Did Man Who Armed the Black Panthers Lead Two Lives?" National Public Radio, October 3, 2012. http://www.npr.org/2012/10/03/161408561/did-man-who-armed-black-panthers-lead-two-lives
3. M. Wesley Swearinger, *FBI Secrets: An Agent Expose* (Boston: South End Press, 1999), 80.
4. Elmer G. Pratt obituary, *New York Times*, June 3, 2011.

Chapter 7

1. Peter Fimrite, "Inside Death Row: At San Quentin, 647 condemned killers wait to die in the most populous execution antechamber in the United States," *San Francisco Chronicle*, November 20, 2005. http://www.sfgate.com/bayarea/article/INSIDE-DEATH-ROW-At-San-Quentin-647-condemned-2594023.php
2. Miles Corwin, "Last Man Executed in California: Furor over Mitchell Case Resounds 18 Years Later," *Los Angeles Times*, August 23, 1985. http://articles.latimes.com/1985-08-23/news/mn-24365_1_aaron-mitchell
3. "History of Capital Punishment in California," California Department of Corrections and Rehabilitation. http://www.cdcr.ca.gov/capital_punishment/history_of_capital_punishment.html
4. Dan Morain, "From Birth to Death Row, Violence Surrounded Harris," *Los Angeles Times*, April 21, 1992. http://articles.latimes.com/1992-04-21/news/mn-608_1_robert-harris

5. Dan Morain, "Witness to the Execution: A Macabre, Surreal Event," *Los Angeles Times*, April 22, 1992. http://articles.latimes .com/1992-04-22/news/mn-509_1_gas-chamber

6. "The Innocence List: List of Those Freed from Death Row," Death Penalty Information Center, September 2, 2014. http:// www.deathpenaltyinfo.org/innocence-list-those-freed-death-row

Chapter 12

1. Louis Fischer, *Gandhi and Stalin* (New York: Harper and Brothers, 1947), 61.

2. "Truth and Reconciliation Commission of South Africa Report, Volumes I-VII," Truth and Reconciliation Commission of South Africa, March 21, 2003. http://www.justice.gov.za/trc/ report/finalreport/Volume%202.pdf

3. Paul Guerino, Paige M. Harrison, and William J. Sabol, Prisoners in 2010, rev. ed. (Washington, DC: Bureau of Justice Statistics, 2011). http://www.bjs.gov/content/pub/pdf/p10.pdf

4. Alexia D. Cooper, Ph.D., Matthew R. Durose, and Howard N. Synder, PhD, *Recidivism of Prisoners Released in 30 States in 2005: Patterns from 2005 to 2010* (Washington, DC: Bureau of Justice Statistics, 2014). http://www.bjs.gov/index.cfm?ty=pb detail&iid=4987

Chapter 13

1. "Elephant Orphanage," *60 Minutes*, CBS, April 9, 2006.

2. Ibid.

3. "Assessment and Evaluation of the IMPACT Program in the Division of Juvenile Justice Facilities in California," California Department of Corrections and Rehabilitation Office of Research, January 2009. http://www.projectimpact.us/pdf /assessment_evaluation.pdf